a HIGHER REALITY
Manifestations of the Unseen

بسم الله الرحمن الرحيم

MOSTAFA AL-BADAWI

WORKS

A Blessed Valley: Wādī Ḥaḍramawt and the ʿAlawī Tradition, Vol. I
Ancient Prophets of Arabia
Man and the Universe
Sufi Sage of Arabia

TRANSLATIONS OF IMĀM ʿABDALLĀH AL-ḤADDĀD'S WORKS

Counsels of Religion
Gifts for the Seeker
Knowledge and Wisdom
The Book of Assistance
The Lives of Man
The Prophetic Invocations
The Sublime Treasures
Two Treatises: Mutual Reminding and Good Manners of the Disciple

TRANSLATION OF ḤABĪB AḤMAD MASHHŪR AL-ḤADDĀD'S WORK

Key to the Garden

TRANSLATION OF SHAYKH ʿABDAL-KHĀLIQ AL-SHABRĀWĪ'S WORK

Degrees of the Soul

TRANSLATION OF SHAYKH USAMA AL-SAYYID MAHMUD AL-AZHARI'S WORK

Introduction to the Principles of Qur'ānic Exegesis

IV

IV Publishing
Email: sales@islamicvillage.co.uk
Website: www.islamicvillage.co.uk

Distributed by HUbooks
Email: info@hubooks.com
Website: www.hubooks.com

Title: A Higher Reality
Author: Moṣṭafā al-Badawī

ISBN: 978-0-9520853-3-1

Editing: Yahya Birt
Proofreading: Andrew Booso
Cover Image: An oil & watercolour painting by Dr Ahmed Moustafa entitled 'The Divine Bedrock of Human Artistry'
Cover Design: Dr Javed Khan

Designed, printed & bound in the United Kingdom by OUTSTANDING
Email: books@outstanding-media.co.uk Tel: +44 (0)121 327 3277

OUTSTANDING

MOSTAFA AL-BADAWI

a HIGHER REALITY

Manifestations *of the Unseen*

Contents

Angels seen by others in their subtle forms
Gabriel appearing in a human form seen only by the Prophet ﷺ
Gabriel seen by others in a human form
Other angels appearing in a human form seen only by the Prophet ﷺ
Angels seen by others in a human form
Witnessing the Angel of Death
Witnessing the angels in the form of birds
The angels as lights (the *Sakīna*)
The Night of Destiny (*Laylat al-Qadr*)
The *Sakīna* appearing in the form of a wind

The speech of animals
The speech of birds and insects
The speech of trees and inanimate things
All created beings glorify their Lord

Introduction

The religious literatures of all world religions contain countless reports of occurrences when ordinarily imperceptible unseen realities intrude into the visible world in a form capable of being seen, heard, touched, smelled, tasted or any combination of these senses. Today, wherever the mentality of the dominant culture prevails, such accounts are as a matter of course considered fictitious or "mythical". Nonetheless, such things have resurfaced in the twentieth and twenty-first centuries through academic interest in paranormal phenomena and extrasensory perception, and popular interest in films depicting them in grotesquely distorted ways. Yet, serious accounts by authoritative religious scholars of varied denominations are still found to be puzzling and hard to believe; however, the very fact that these phenomena are widely reported and so ubiquitous makes it difficult simply to dismiss them.

We are watching the West firmly set on a breathless race toward what it perceives as freedom, which in reality amounts to no more than freedom from religious constraints. Religion necessarily means both a clearly intelligible faith and conformity to a Divinely-revealed sacred law. Today, we see many people whose faith has become a form of vague sentimental attachment that is no longer capable of answering their basic existential questions. Unlike their own ancestors, they no longer feel the need to conform to a Divine law to regulate their behaviour. The inevitable endpoint of such attitudes is either virtual or explicit atheism and the complete loss of self-control masquerading as freedom. In such a climate, the unseen realities not capable of being perceived by such atrophied senses or captured by one gadget or another will simply be dismissed as fantasy. For example, the electrical impulses produced by the brains of certain spiritual people are being studied, but only in an attempt to confirm the preconceived materialistic notion that "the mind is what the brain does". Once one realises that the material world with all its visible and invisible energies is but an infinitesimal portion of the universe, the absurdity of such projects becomes evident.

Nowadays, it is this kind of scepticism which sadly pervades vast tracts of the planet, not only through the media and the internet, but through all kinds of educational and research institutions to such an extent that many minds, Muslims and others, suffer from the inevitable contamination. The result is that Muslims are gradually becoming more and more materialistic in their thinking and attitudes, which is demonstrably damaging their ability to understand and practise their religion to the required depth. Yet in Islām, it is essential to have faith in the Unseen; and furthermore, it can never be divorced from practical conformity with the Sacred Law.

However, Muslims, of all people, being in possession of a complete theory of the Unseen, should have no reservations about fully accepting unseen realities, with the only proviso being that they are reliably reported. The dimension that bridges the gap between the corporeal world and the pure spiritual world and contains such events is termed *ʿĀlam al-Mithāl* by Muslim scholars, tentatively translated as the World of Similitudes, or sometimes as the Imaginal World or *Mundus Imaginalis* by Western authors.

The World of Similitudes is referred to in the works of many great and authoritative Muslim scholars. It is mentioned for instance by Qur'ānic commentators such as Abu'l-Suʿūd al-ʿImādī, Alūsī, Ismāʿīl Ḥaqqī, Ibn ʿAjība, and more recently Ibn ʿĀshūr and by many *muḥaddithūn* or traditionists, such as Imām Suyūṭī in his commentary on the *Muwaṭṭa'* of Imām Mālik, Imām Munāwī in his commentary on *al-Jāmiʿ al-Ṣaghīr* and Sindī in his commentary of the *Sunan* of Ibn Māja. As for the Sufis, they take it for granted and write about it profusely in their works.

The term "similitude" refers to the fact that these normally invisible realities appear in an equivalent form in the visible world; this form is a similitude of the reality in question. To give an example, we know that everything that flies in the air must necessarily possess wings. Therefore, every being, such as the angels, that moves freely in the subtle world possesses something equivalent to wings in this one and fly in what is the equivalent of air here. When angels appear in a form, whether subtle or physical, this faculty will appear in the worldly form that corresponds to it, which is wings. This law of correspondence is what permitted the Prophet ﷺ to say that spirits meet and recognise each other in the air.[1] We know that the world in which spirits move about has no air like earth's, which is composed of nitrogen, oxygen and carbon dioxide. What is meant is that there is a medium that corresponds to air in the physical world. When there is no material air, there is obviously no need for material wings. Nevertheless, the Qur'ān describes the angels as Divine messengers possessing two, three or four pairs of wings.[2] Moreover, when the Prophet ﷺ described the descent of Jesus at the end of time, he said he would alight near the white minaret in Damascus, his hands resting on the wings of the angels.[3] He also described to his Companions his own cousin Jaʿfar, following his death at the Battle of Mu'ta, as flying through the air with wings, so that he became known among them as Jaʿfar al-Ṭayyār, the Flyer. Now we know that Jaʿfar's spirit has no material wings with which to fly through material air, so that which appeared to the Prophet ﷺ in the World of Similitudes as visible wings was an intelligible meaning, that of flying through the air, in a form recognisable as such by the human senses, which is that of wings.

Manifestations from the World of Similitudes are often, but not always, visual. The images seen can be subtle, and more or less transparent; for example, when the Prophet ﷺ was shown Paradise and Hell in the wall before him; and these manifestations resemble the images seen in dreams. Or these images can be dense and heavy and fully materialised; for instance, when Gabriel (Jibrīl) appeared to the Prophet ﷺ in a physical form resembling that of his Companion Diḥya al-Kalbī, a form that not only could be seen, but also heard and touched. These manifestations can also be voices heard by the physical ear, odours smelt by the physical nose, or flavours such as nectar or milk that can be tasted by the tongue. Examples of the first are the voices of the angels that the Prophets and the saints hear without seeing them, those of babies such as Jesus speaking, those of animals, birds, and insects speaking in human languages, those of mountains and pebbles glorifying God, palm trunks weeping, and the resonating bell that the Prophet ﷺ heard as the Qur'ān was being revealed. We know that lifeless matter, plants, animals, and human babies are normally unable to produce intelligible speech that our physical ears can hear. Nevertheless, as mentioned earlier, there have been innumerable reports of such occurrences in every culture and civilisation since the dawn of history. These are invisible intelligible realities that are brought out into the visible material world through what is considered an extraordinary or miraculous process so that they are clearly perceived by the senses; and this is the World of Similitudes.

This World of Similitudes is in no way illusory: to the contrary, it is more real than the physical world and is fully capable of affecting events on earth. Examples of such occurrences that have transformed the course of events in the material world are the descent of Gabriel with the Qur'ān, which resulted in the birth of the Islamic religion, his showing the Muslims the way to the fort of Banī Qurayẓa, and the descent of the angels from the third heaven on the Day of Badr, when they appeared in human form as turbaned warriors on horseback and fought alongside the Muslim army. They were seen by the Prophet ﷺ, the Muslims and the pagans, wreaking havoc with very real swords and whips. On these occasions they appeared in human form, not in their subtle winged forms.

At other times, such as the Night of Destiny (*Laylat al-Qadr*) and in response to Qur'ān recitation, angels appear as a cloud of lights from which is heard a humming sound resembling that of bees. This manifestation is called the Peace (*Sakīna*), because its descent appeases distraught hearts, pacifies anguished minds, and makes one feel the presence of the Lord, experiencing such profound contentment that one's dearest wish is that this state should endure forever. The Peace is thus one of the powers or forces acting at God's bidding and doing His work. It usually remains unseen and descends into the hearts of the believers. The Qur'ān says, ***He it is who sent down the Peace into the hearts of the believers, that they may increase in faith over their faith, and to God belongs the hosts of the heavens and the earth, and God is Knowing, Wise.***[4] Moreover, the Prophet ﷺ said, "*No people shall ever gather to remember God but the angels shall surround them, mercy envelops them, the Peace (Sakīna) descends upon them, and God mentions them to those with Him.*"[5] Many of the Companions reported the manifestation of the *Sakīna* when revelation descended into the heart of the Prophet ﷺ, at which time he became very heavy and his she-camel was forced to kneel down under the weight.[6]

In addition, the *Sakīna* is established as descending into the hearts of saints, the pure-hearted people of God, who speak from inspiration at such moments when they speak. Although the words come out of their mouths, they are usually aware that the discourse is not really theirs. During his caliphate, it is reported that Imām ʿAlī once asked those around him, "Who is the best of this community after its Prophet?" They answered, "You, O Commander of the Faithful." He said, "Not so, but Abū Bakr, then ʿUmar. It is not at all unlikely that the Peace speaks on the tongue of ʿUmar."[7] He thereby indicated that the reality of the *Sakīna* included the angels of inspiration casting into the hearts of people such as ʿUmar knowledge that then appears in their utterances. The Prophet ﷺ had already said that just as there had been Divinely-inspired people in previous communities, so there were in his, and foremost among them was ʿUmar.[8] But the *Sakīna* also sometimes manifests outwardly and becomes perceptible to the senses; and it was again ʿAlī who described how the Peace came in the form of a cloud that led Abraham to Makka and indicated to him exactly where to build the Kaʿba.[9]

Manifestations from the World of Similitudes may also be seen during sleep, when a person's physical senses withdraw from the physical world and the soul is entirely free to concentrate on the Unseen. In this circumstance, these manifestations are called dream-visions. The third possibility is for them to be seen in one of the intermediate states that occur between sleep and full consciousness and they are then called the Major Event (*Wāqiʿa*). On such occasions, perception is with the sensors of the heart, not those of the body.

A good example of a single event that demonstrates a variety of manifestations from the World of Similitudes is the Prophet's birth. Ibn ʿAbbās is reported to have said that Lady Āmina, the Prophet's mother, had said that she had been alone at home when the pains of labour started. Suddenly, she heard a tumult that terrified her. Then she glimpsed the wing of a white bird pass over her heart, assuaging her and removing her pain. She then noticed beside her a white beverage, which she thought was milk. As she was thirsty, she drank it, and immediately saw a light shine out of her up to the sky. Soon afterwards she saw tall women standing around her, assisting her with the childbirth.[10] These are three examples of normally unseen subtle realities appearing in the material world to perform specific functions. She also reported that the night before, her sight had become acute and she was able to see distant lands from east to west. Other reported manifestations of subtle realities witnessed that night include the light that illuminated everything in the room and the light that shone forth from the lady's womb with the appearance of the blessed newborn baby, which made her see the palaces of Syria. We have several authenticated reports that during childbirth she saw a light that illuminated places as far as the Byzantine palaces of Syria, which she was able actually to see and describe.[11] ʿUthmān ibn Abi'l-ʿĀṣ, whose mother had attended upon the Lady Āmina during childbirth and witnessed the Prophet's birth, relates that he had heard her say that there was nothing on that night that she looked at in the house that did not shine with light and that she saw the stars draw so near that she felt they were about to fall down on her.[12]

Among other properties, the World of Similitudes can show events that are long gone or are yet to happen. An example of this is that of the Prophet ﷺ seeing ancient Prophets travelling through the wilderness of the Ḥijāz. It has been reliably reported that he once asked Abū Bakr as they travelled together, "*Which valley is this?*" Upon being told that it was the valley of ʿUsfān, he said, "*Hūd and Ṣāliḥ passed through here on red camels with fibre bridles, rough cloths around their waists and striped ones around their shoulders, saying the* talbiya, *heading for the Ancient House on pilgrimage.*"[13]

He also saw things that had yet to happen both in this world and in the Hereafter, for he saw and described in great detail the events at the end of time; and he also saw during his Ascension (*Miʿrāj*) the punishment of many kinds of sinners in Hell, which is a matter that will only come about after the Day of Judgement.

During the course of his Ascension, the Prophet ﷺ noticed some turbulence in the Terrestrial Heaven. He saw smoke and heard noises, so he asked Gabriel what it was, and was told that these were devils hovering over the eyes of men to prevent them from meditating on the dominion of the heavens and the earth, for otherwise they would see wonders.[14]

We may conclude from this and previous episodes that certain people in certain circumstances may witness what is hidden from the majority at one or more of the many levels of reality, either in full wakefulness, asleep, or in an intermediate state between the two. When this witnessing is in the waking state it is called "unveiling", whether it is a manifestation from the World of Similitudes appearing in this one or the reality of a material thing or event that is invisible to others because of its remoteness. An example to illustrate the latter is when the Prophet ﷺ saw what was happening to his Companions at the Battle of Mu'ta in present-day Jordan, and described it as it happened to his Companions who were with him in Madina.

As soon as a person closes his eyes, he ordinarily begins to see a constant flow of images and scenes in his mind. This is the World of Imagination. These images are subtle not concrete, possess neither density nor mass, are not subject to time or space, and undergo unceasing change. Once we grasp these attributes of the subtle images, we can better understand their appearance in similar forms in all subtle dimensions and how intelligible meanings appear in the same form in the World of Dreams and in the World of Similitudes. The degree of subtlety of the images varies according to their level in the subtle world's hierarchy. The higher we go the subtler the images are, until we pass through all the dimensions of subtle images and reach the dimensions of formless realities, where there are no longer any forms but just lights or intelligible meanings, which may also be called "spirits". These are beyond form and are evidently not subject to time or space as we know them.

Now an intelligible reality in the world of meanings, spirits or lights is formless, but when it descends to the Intermediary World (*Malakūt*), the world of subtle images, it becomes clothed in the form appropriate to the level it has descended to. When an intelligible reality reaches the physical world, it becomes clothed in a solid form perceivable by the physical senses.

A good example to understand this is human communication. It occurs through a sequence of events that begins with an intelligible meaning occurring in the mind. This thought then summons visual images from the memory to clothe it and the imagination is thus set into motion, and we are now in the world of imaginary images. The third stage is the appearance of this intelligible reality in the outside world, clothed in the medium capable of expressing it, which is speech travelling as sound waves, to be received by the apparatus necessary to receive them, which is the ear.

The subtle dimension has a negative side and this side appears in nightmares. These disturbing dreams are products of one's imagination and are often accompanied by an unsettling emotional state. These have no higher reality and are illusory.

Dreams of all kinds can occur as we are going to sleep or waking up but not as yet fully awake. At such times, because we are half-conscious, they are perceived as hallucinations, as mental images that appear to be external, although they are seen in one's mind. For psychologists, hypnopompic dreams are those that occur when one is in the process of waking up but is not fully awake, while hypnagogic dreams are those that happen when one is falling sleep, but is not yet fully asleep. Neither kind is relevant spiritually or psychiatrically. It is only when they occur in a full waking state that they are considered to be definitely pathological, for these are usually psychotic symptoms that require treatment. Thus, to perceive subtle images from one's own imagination projected outward as if into the objective external space can be normal in hypnopompic or hypnagogic states or abnormal in psychotic illnesses, under the influence of hallucinogenic drugs, organic diseases of the brain, or in certain infrequent hysterical states.

To perceive subtle images clearly from the ordinarily invisible dimensions in one's half - or fully - awake state is normal, but not ordinary in as much as only the élite are given to experience such occurrences regularly, while ordinary people may do so only once or twice in a lifetime. There is thus a grey area between the normal and the pathological domains, which has given rise to many misinterpretations.

We shall begin our journey – God willing – with the World of Dream-visions, then proceed to study the World of Similitudes by quoting sufficient evidence from the Qur'ān, the *Sunna* and the recorded histories of the men of God to render the subject abundantly clear. We have divided the section on the World of Similitudes into titled subsections in an attempt to add some clarity to a subject that is by nature complex, multidimensional and open-ended. There is of course considerable overlap between the subsections, and many of the events quoted under one title could equally well have been cited under several other titles.

PART ONE

The World of Dreams

I

Kinds of Dreams

According to the Prophet ﷺ, there are three kinds of dreams: one that is inspired by God or the angel, a second that originates within the soul and where the sleeper sees ordinary events and people in his life, and a third that is chaotic and sometimes terrifying and comes from the lower demonic worlds. The Prophet ﷺ said, "*When the time approaches, the vision of a Muslim shall hardly ever lie. The most truthful in speech among you is the most truthful in vision. The vision of a Muslim is one forty-sixth* [*of the attributes*] *of prophecy. Visions are of three kinds: a good vision that is good news from God; a vision that aggrieves and is from the Devil; and a vision of what one thinks within oneself. Should you see something that displeases you, rise to your feet and pray, and then say nothing about it to anyone.*"[15]

Here is an example of the demonic dream: The Prophet's Companion Jābir said, "A man came to the Prophet ﷺ as he was preaching, and said to him, 'O Messenger of God, I saw last night in my sleep that my neck was cut off and my head rolled down; so I followed it, took it, and placed it back in its place.' The Messenger of God ﷺ said, '*When the Devil toys with one of you in his dream, speak of it to no one.*'"[16]

DREAM-VISIONS ARE ONE PART OF PROPHECY

The Prophet ﷺ informs us that dream-visions are one part of Prophecy that is to remain with the Muslim community until the end of time. Most *ḥadīths* declare it to be a forty-sixth part of Prophecy; some make it a twenty-fifth, a fiftieth or a seventieth. Much has been said by scholars over the years to explain this, but the truth is that such things are known only to the Prophets, who have to reveal them to us if we are to understand them in depth; and as they have not, no amount of speculation will provide us with final answers. The Prophet ﷺ said, "*Good conduct, good bearing, and economy are a twenty-fifth part of Prophecy.*"[17]

He said that it was a seventieth part of Prophecy to delay *suḥūr*, hasten with breaking one's fast, and point one's finger during the ritual prayer.[18] Now the first *ḥadīth* speaks of general trends in outward appearance and actions, while the second speaks of specific single actions. As for those mentioning dream-visions, they are concerned with things occurring inwardly in one's mind. It is therefore likely that each *ḥadīth* is concerned with a different system of division of the parts of Prophecy.

For years, the Prophet ﷺ was in the habit of asking his Companions each morning after the prayer whether any of them had seen a dream. Any of them who had seen a dream he thought was worth recounting would come forward and tell him about it.[19]

WHAT TO DO AFTER SEEING A DREAM

The Prophet ﷺ advised his Companions that if one has a good dream one should thank God and consider it good news from Him, and relate it only to those considered worthy. But he who sees something in a dream that he dislikes should blow thrice to his left side[i], get up, do his ritual ablutions, pray and ask God for protection against the evil in it, then not mention it to anyone. In this manner, it would not harm him.[20]

The reason why bad dreams should not be talked about is that the bad event a dream contains remains contained in the invisible world, and only when one talks about it, as the Prophet ﷺ warned, do the barriers holding it back become unlocked and it becomes free to actually come to pass in the material world. If no mention is made of a bad dream, or if it is mentioned only to a learned or wise person, and protection is sought from God against its evil, it does not cross over into the material dimension.[21] This had actually happened in the Prophet's time. ʿĀ'isha, the Prophet's wife, recounted how there was a woman in Madina whose husband was a merchant. He was often away and frequently left her pregnant, and each time he did this she saw the same dream. She used to come to the Prophet ﷺ to recount her dream, say-

i The Arabic word used in the ḥadīth is *Yatful*, which means blowing with a "Tuff! Tuff!" noise like spitting, but dryly without actual spittle.

ing, "My husband has gone to trade, leaving me pregnant. I saw in my dream that the pillar of my house has been broken and that I had given birth to a one-eyed boy." The Prophet ﷺ said, "*Good, your husband will return to you – God willing – in a good state and you will give birth to an affectionate boy.*" Her husband would then return safely and she would give birth to a boy. One day she came as she used to do, but found that the Prophet ﷺ was not there. 'Ā'isha inquired what it was about, but she said she preferred to wait to tell the Prophet ﷺ. However, 'Ā'isha insisted so much that she told her of her dream. She interpreted it to mean that her husband would die and she would give birth to an evil boy, at which the woman began to cry. Soon afterwards the Prophet ﷺ walked in and enquired what the matter was. When 'Ā'isha told him how she had interpreted the dream, he was displeased and told her that when she interprets a dream for a Muslim she must give it the best possible interpretation, for it shall occur just as it was interpreted.[22]

The purpose of quoting the following dreams is not to explore the science of dream interpretation, but to compare them with the visions of the World of Similitude and understand that the two worlds are virtually identical and the stuff of which they are made is the same, except that one occurs in the sleeping state and internally, while the other occurs in the waking state and externally.

DREAM-VISIONS IN THE QUR'ĀN

The dreams of perfect men, such as the Prophets, the Divine Envoys, are entirely true. However, they are still of several kinds. Imām Rāzī in his Qur'ān commentary states that the dreams of the Prophets are of three kinds. The first kind comes to pass exactly as it was seen. An example of that is when the Prophet ﷺ saw that he entered the Sacred Mosque in Makka, which happened some time later. The other two kinds require interpretation, for in one what actually happens is the opposite of what is seen, as when Abraham saw that he was being ordered to slaughter his son, but when the event came to pass it was the ram that was slaughtered instead and his son was saved. The third kind requires interpretation because it is symbolic, as the vision of Joseph who saw eleven stars and the sun and the moon prostrating before him.[23]

ABRAHAM'S VISION

In the Qur'ān, Abraham says, ***I shall go to my Lord and He shall guide me.*** He then addresses his Lord thus, ***Lord, grant me one of the virtuous!*** God responds by promising him a boy of exceptional wisdom and the story unfolds as follows, ***So We gave him glad tidings of a sagacious boy. When he was able to hasten with him, he said, "My son, I have seen in my dream that I am sacrificing you; so see what you think." He said, "My father, do as you are commanded, you shall find me – God willing – one who is steadfast."***[24] Abraham said this after he was saved from the fire of Nimrod, for he decided to leave the land of idolatry and emigrate to where his Lord would guide him, which turned out to be Palestine. When he reached the Holy Land, he asked for a virtuous son. He was given the glad news that he would be granted a son who would live long enough to be recognised as a sage. Then when the boy was old enough to accompany his father when going about his business, he was commanded in his dream to sacrifice him. Since the dream-visions of Divine Envoys pertain to revelation, Abraham had no hesitation in obeying and his son Ishmael had no option but to comply with the Divine command.

JOSEPH'S VISION

In his dream, Joseph saw eleven planets and the sun and moon prostrating before him. He had eleven brothers, so he interpreted the eleven planets as representing his brothers. He interpreted the sun as representing his father and the moon his stepmother Leah, for his mother had died giving birth to his brother Benjamin and he was raised by his stepmother.

2

Dream-visions of the Prophet ﷺ and his Companions

As for the dream-visions of our Prophet ﷺ, he saw premonitory dreams before the battles of Badr and Uḥud, and before the Day of Ḥudaybiya.

VISION OF THE DAY OF BADR

As for Badr, the Qur'ān says, ***When God showed them to you in your dream as few; had He shown them to you as many, you would have lost heart and quarrelled about the matter; but God saved. He knows the thoughts in the breasts. When He showed them you in your eyes when you met as few and made you few in their eyes, that God may decide a matter that was done. To God do all things return.***[25] And it did happen that when the Prophet ﷺ fell into a light sleep he saw the enemy, but he saw the reality of the situation, that their numbers will avail them nothing and they were to be defeated as the events of the day unfolded as if they were few in number. He informed his Companions of this, which encouraged them greatly.

VISION OF THE DAY OF UḤUD

When the Prophet ﷺ was still in Makka, he saw that he would emigrate to a land of palms, which he thought might be Yamāma or Ḥajar,[i] but it turned out to be Madina. He also saw in the same dream that he was shaking a sword and that its blade was broken, which foretold what would befall the believers on the Day of Uḥud. He then shook the sword again and it changed to being better than it was originally, which

---

i Yamāma was where present-day Riyadh now stands, while Ḥajar used to be on the Arabian shores of the Arabian Gulf.

meant that the believers would rally after Uḥud and that God would eventually grant them victory.[26] In the same dream, the Prophet ﷺ also saw himself dressed in sturdy armour and there were slaughtered cattle around him; he interpreted the armour to be Madina and the cattle as his martyred Companions.[27]

VISION OF JESUS AND THE ANTICHRIST

The Prophet ﷺ saw the Dajjāl, the Impostor or Antichrist of the end of time, and also Jesus, son of Mary.

VISION OF THE IMPOSTORS OF YEMEN AND OF YAMĀMA

The Prophet ﷺ once saw two gold bracelets on his wrists, which he disliked, as wearing gold was forbidden to men under Sacred Law. He was inspired in his dream to blow on them and so blew them away. He interpreted this as meaning that two impostors would appear after him; subsequently, they did appear as al-Aswad al-ʿAnasī, the impostor of Yemen, and Musaylima, the impostor of Yamāma.[28]

RELIGION APPEARING AS A TUNIC

The Prophet ﷺ said, "*As I was asleep, I was shown the people and they were wearing tunics, some down to their breasts, some longer. I was shown ʿUmar and he wore a tunic that dragged on the ground.*" They asked him, "How did you interpret it, O Messenger of God?" He answered, "*Religion.*"[29]

KNOWLEDGE APPEARING AS MILK

On another occasion the Prophet ﷺ said, "*As I was asleep, I drank milk to such satiety that I saw it ooze out of my fingernails. Then I passed it to ʿUmar.*" They asked him, "How did you interpret it?" He answered, "*Knowledge.*"[30]

In the first dream, the intelligible reality that is religion appeared in the form of a tunic, while in the second another intelligible reality, namely knowledge, appeared in the form of milk. Both dreams required interpretation, as their true meaning was different from their manifestation.

FEVER APPEARING AS A WOMAN

When the Prophet ﷺ arrived to Madina following his flight from Makka, he found the people to be suffering from recurrent malaria-like fevers that had plagued them for as long as they could remember. He implored his Lord to remove it from Madina and send it far south to Juḥfa. Following this, he saw in his dream a dishevelled black woman hastening out of Madina and reaching Juḥfa. He interpreted it as the fever being expelled from Madina.[31]

SEEING FRIDAY AND THE REALITY OF THIS WORLD

The Prophet ﷺ also said that he was shown the days of the week as if in a mirror and was impressed with the light and radiance of Friday. Then he noticed a black spot, asked what it was, and he was told that it was on a Friday that the Hour would come.[32] He ﷺ said, "*The world came to me, young and fair, and raised her head and adorned herself for me, so I said, 'I do not want you.' She said, 'Even if you escape me, others will not.'*"[33] In these dream-visions we see two intelligible concepts, Friday and this world, appearing in visible form, the first as a mirror with a black spot and the other as a fair young maid.

He ﷺ is also reported to have said, "*The first and the last were shown to me in my quarters last night.*" Someone asked, "O Messenger of God, those who have gone by?" He said, "*Yes, Adam and those after him.*" They asked, "And those who were in the loins of men and the wombs of women?" "He said, "*Yes, their likeness was modelled for me in mud and I recognised them, just as Adam was taught all the names.*"[34]

EATING DATES IN A DREAM

The Prophet ﷺ said, "*I saw that I had been brought a lump of dates and that I chewed it in my mouth, and there was a stone in it which hurt me, so I spat it out. Then I took another lump, chewed it, found a stone in it, and spat it out. Then I took another lump, chewed it, found a stone in it, and spat it out.*" Abū Bakr said, "Allow me to interpret it." "*Interpret it then,*" he said. Abū Bakr interpreted it as indicating that one of the Prophet's armies sent on expedition would return safely and with booty, and that three times they would meet a man who would claim to be under the Prophet's protection, and on all three occasions they would let him go. The Prophet ﷺ said, "*Thus did the angel say,*"[35] meaning this was how the angel interpreted the dream.

VISION OF THE RELIGIOUS COMMUNITIES ON THE DAY OF JUDGEMENT

The Prophet ﷺ once said, "*The communities were shown to me; there was a Prophet going by accompanied by one man, another by two men, a Prophet with a group, and another with no one. I saw a large crowd covering the entire horizon. I hoped this would be my community, but I was told, 'This is Moses and his community.' Then I was told, 'Look!' And I saw a large crowd covering the entire horizon. Then I was told, 'Look this side and that side,' and I saw a large crowd covering the entire horizon, and it was said to me, 'This is your community and with it are seventy thousand who will enter Paradise without prior judgement.'*"[36]

VISIONS OF THE COMPANIONS INTERPRETED BY THE PROPHET ﷺ

When one of the Companions saw in his dream a cloud dripping butter and honey, the cloud was interpreted by Abū Bakr as Islām and the butter and honey as the Qur'ān.[37] This interpretation means that Islām is conceived of as shading its adherents like a cloud and raining upon them the verses of the Qur'ān which are as sweet as honey and as soft as butter.

We know that the *adhān*, the call to the prayer, was simultaneously seen in a dream by ʿUmar and a man of the Anṣār and that the latter was first to inform the Prophet ﷺ.[38]

ʿĀ'isha once said, "I saw three moons falling into my apartment." The Prophet ﷺ said, "*If your dream is true, three persons who are the best on earth will be buried in your apartment.*" When he died and was buried in her apartment her father Abū Bakr said to her, "This is the first of your moons and the best."[39]

DREAM-VISIONS OF THE PROPHET ﷺ AND HIS COMPANIONS

ʿAbdallāh ibn ʿUmar said that in the days of the Prophet ﷺ whenever someone saw a vision he would relate it to him. He therefore wished to see a dream-vision so as to have something to relate to the Prophet ﷺ. At that time he was a young boy and used to sleep in the Prophet's mosque. One night he saw that two angels were taking him to the Fire and that it was lined with stones like a well usually is, and that it had two horns, and there were people in there whom he knew. He began repeating, "I seek God's protection from the Fire!" Then another angel came saying, "Have no fear." He recounted the dream to his sister Ḥafṣa, the Prophet's wife, who in turn recounted it to the Prophet ﷺ, whose only comment was, "*What a good man ʿAbdallāh is, were he only to pray at night.*" After this episode, ʿAbdallāh was known to sleep very little during the night.[40]

ʿAbdallāh ibn Salām was said to be a man destined for the Garden. When questioned about it, he said that the reason was that in the Prophet's time he had seen a dream and narrated it to the Prophet ﷺ. ʿAbdallāh had seen himself in a wide green garden at the centre of which was an iron pillar, the lower end of which rested on the ground, while the upper end was in heaven. At its upper tip was a handle. He was bid to climb, but said he could not, so a groom came and helped him up until he reached the top and grasped the handle. He was then told to hold it firmly. When he recounted the dream to the Prophet ﷺ, he was told, "*The garden is Islām, the pillar is the pillar of Islām, and the handle is the Firm Handle. You shall be steadfast in Islām until you die.*"[41]

Abū Bakr said that one day the Prophet ﷺ asked them who had seen a dream and a man said that he had seen scales coming down from the sky, then the Prophet ﷺ was weighed against Abū Bakr and outweighed him. Then Abū Bakr was weighed against ʿUmar and outweighed him. Then ʿUmar was weighed against ʿUthmān and outweighed him. Then the scales were lifted up again. The Prophet's face expressed displeasure, then he said, "*This is the succession of Prophethood, then God shall give sovereignty to whomsoever He will.*"[42]

SEEING THE PROPHET ﷺ IN DREAM-VISIONS

The Prophet ﷺ said, "*He who has seen me in his sleep will see me when awake. The Devil does not assume my form.*"[43] and he said, "*He who has seen me has seen the truth, for the Devil cannot look like me.*"[44]

Al-Rabīʿ ibn Sulaymān, one of the foremost disciples of Imām Shāfiʿī, said that as they were in Egypt Shāfiʿī gave him a letter and asked him to take it to Imām Aḥmad ibn Ḥanbal in Baghdad. He took it and travelled to Iraq. He found Imām Aḥmad sitting in the *miḥrāb* after the dawn prayer, so he waited until the Imām got up and prepared to go, then he approached him saying, "This is a letter from your brother Shāfiʿī in Egypt." He asked him, "Did you read it?" He said, "No", so he broke the seal, read it and his eyes were filled with tears. Al-Rabīʿ asked him, "What is it, O Abū ʿAbdallāh?" he said, "He says he saw the Prophet ﷺ in his sleep and he told him, "*Write to Abū ʿAbdallāh, give him greetings of peace and tell him, 'You will be tested and asked to confirm the creation of the Qur'ān. Do not obey them and God will raise your banner until the Day of Resurrection.*'" Al-Rabīʿ asked him for a gift for the good news, so the imām removed one of his tunics, the one next to his skin, gave it to him, and gave him his answer to Imām Shāfiʿī. When he returned to Egypt and handed it to him, he asked him, "What did he give you?" He answered, "His tunic." Shāfiʿī said, "We shall not distress you by taking it from you, but dip it in water and give me the water so that I may seek its blessing."[45] Shāfiʿī is known to have washed his face with this water every morning.

Illustrious traditionists such as Ibn ʿAsākir and Dhahabī have reported that three of the earlier great traditionists of the fourth century of the Hijra – Ibn al-Muqri', Abu'l-Shaykh, and Ṭabarānī – were once in Madina together.[i] They had run out of money and were at a loss for what to do. They went without food for a day and a night. When things became difficult, Ibn al-Muqri' stood before the Prophet's grave and said, "O Messenger of God, hunger!" Ṭabarānī said to him, "Sit down! It is either one of two things: we shall be given provision or we shall die." Sometime afterward a *sharīf* from Madina presented himself at the door accompanied by two servants carrying baskets of provisions. He said, "You have complained about me to the Prophet ﷺ. I saw him

---

i All three are still acknowledged to this day as great scholars and traditionists (*muḥaddithūn*).

in my sleep and he has ordered me to bring something to you."

Dhahabī reports yet another such story in his biography of Ibn al-Muqri'. Ismā'īl ibn 'Abbād, a minister of the Buwayhid sultans, was a learned man who liked the company of scholars. He was once asked, "You are a man of Mu'tazilite thought and Ibn al-Muqri' is a traditionist. How is it that you are so fond of him?" He answered that Ibn al-Muqri' had been his father's friend and that once, when he was asleep, he saw the Prophet ﷺ saying to him, "Do you sleep, when one of God's saints is at your door?" He awoke to find Abū Bakr ibn al-Muqri' at his door.[46]

SEEING GOD IN DREAM-VISIONS

Ibn 'Abbās said that he heard the Prophet ﷺ say, "*My Lord came to me last night in the best of appearances* (I think he said, "*in my dream*") *and said, 'O Muḥammad, do you know what the Supreme Assembly is arguing about?' I said, 'No.' So He placed His hand between my shoulder blades so that I felt the cool of it between my breasts* (or he might have said, "*in the bottom of my neck*") *and I knew what is in the heavens and the earth. He said, 'O Muḥammad, do you know what the Supreme Assembly is arguing about?' I said, 'Yes, about deeds of expiation.'*"[47]

Now it is obviously impossible for the Absolute to have an appearance that can be seen, so what did the Prophet ﷺ see? When God is seen in a dream-vision, He appears under a form He creates for the purpose and uses to announce His presence, and causes the form to appear accompanied by utter certainty as to its identity. This form functions somewhat like a street sign that announces that this is a particular street, while being neither the street itself nor being able to give an accurate picture of how the street looks.

VISIONS OF THE COMPANIONS AFTER THE PROPHET'S DEPARTURE

'Umar ibn al-Khaṭṭāb was once delivering his regular Friday sermon, wherein he mentioned the Prophet ﷺ and Abū Bakr, and then he said, "I have seen a cockerel pecking me three times. I think this is nothing but that my time has come." He is reported to have specified that it was a red cockerel and when he recounted it to Asmā' bint 'Umays, Abū Bakr's widow, she said he would be killed by a Persian. When Wednesday came he was stabbed.[48]

Al-Ḥasan, 'Alī's son, saw the Prophet ﷺ holding on to the Throne, Abū Bakr holding on to his hips, 'Umar holding on to Abū Bakr's hips, and 'Uthmān holding on to 'Umar's hips. He then saw blood raining from the sky to the earth. He related this in the presence of some of the Shī'a and they asked, "Did you not see 'Alī?" He answered, "There is none I would have loved more to see holding on to the Prophet's hips than 'Alī, but this is the dream-vision I had."[49]

Anas saw 'Abdallāh ibn 'Umar eating dates. He wrote to him, "I saw you eating dates and this – God willing – is the sweetness of faith."[50]

PART TWO

The World of Imagination

The imagination is one of the psyche's most powerful elements when it corresponds to reality and not to mere fantasy. When an image of reality is present in the imagination with sufficient force it can motivate a person to take up a particular kind of behaviour. To give an example, one may read the description of Paradise in the Qur'ān but remain indifferent, thinking of it as something remote and not of immediate relevance to the present moment. Or to the contrary, the description may arouse vivid images in the imagination that drive a person to adopt a certain course of action in order to attain Paradise in the Hereafter. Alternatively, one may read descriptions of Hell and remain unaffected, thinking it unlikely to exist, or one may perceive it vividly in one's imagination and immediately desist from whatever sinful behaviour one is engaged in to avoid being punished for it in the Hereafter.

We know that certainty is conceived by Muslim scholars as having three *degrees*. The first, the Knowledge of Certainty, consists in knowledge accepted with so much conviction that it cannot be shaken by doubt. This conviction depends entirely on the imagination. The second kind is the Eye or Vision of Certainty, which is actually to see the thing itself. The third is the Truth of Certainty, which is to come so near to the thing that not only can it be seen, but also touched, heard, or smelled.

This classification is important in understanding certain passages of the Qur'ān. *Sūra al-Takāthur* is a good example: ***Rivalry distracts you until you visit the graves. No! You shall come to know! Again No, you shall come to know! No, had you known the knowledge of certainty, you would have seen Hell. Again, you shall surely see it with the vision of certainty, then on that day you shall be questioned about what you enjoyed.***[51] The rivalry in question is competition and boasting about wealth and children. Those in whose minds such concerns are paramount are incapable of attending to their state in the

Hereafter, especially if this boasting continues until they die and go to their graves. Their sojourn in the grave is called a ***visit*** because they will soon be resurrected for the Day of Judgement, so their passage in the graves is temporary. The first ***No! You shall come to know!*** refers to their being shown their seats in Hell after death. The second ***You shall come to know!*** refers to their vision of Hell on the Day of Resurrection. Now had they had the Knowledge of Certainty, they would have seen Hell in their imagination with an imaginary vision so intense that it would have driven them to act on it. But they had no such certainty and consequently they are to see Hell again, but this time with the Vision of Certainty on the Day of Resurrection. Thus, it can be seen how sound imagination in this world may save people from the Fire and lead them to the Garden in the Next Life.

In the Prophet's time, there was a young man in Madina by the name of Ḥāritha who was given to arduous devotional and ascetic practices. Upon meeting him one day, the Prophet ﷺ asked him, "*How are you today, Ḥāritha?*" The young man answered, "I am truly a believer, O Messenger of God." The Prophet ﷺ said, "*For every truth there is a reality. What is the reality of your faith?*" He answered, "My soul has turned away from the world so that gold and dust have become equal in my sight. I have made my days thirsty and my nights sleepless. It is as if the Throne of my Lord and the Garden and its people visiting each other and the Fire and its people screaming to each other are made apparent to me." What this means is that this young man of Madina had become so detached from this world that dust and gold had become the same for him, which is a very high degree of detachment. His days are thirsty because he is fasting and his nights are sleepless because he spends them in prayer. He is so intent upon the Hereafter that he can almost see the Divine Throne made manifest on the Day of Judgement, the people of Paradise in their beatitude and the people of Hell in their suffering. The Prophet ﷺ accepted the entire declaration from him, saying, "*A believer whose heart God has enlightened.*" Or, as in other versions, "*Now you know, so remain steadfast!*"[52]

Ḥanẓala al-Usaydī, one the Prophet's scribes, said that he was rushing thought the streets of Madina one day when he met Abū Bakr, who asked him how he was. He said, "Ḥanẓala has become a hypocrite!"

Abū Bakr exclaimed, "Transcendent is God! What are you saying?" He said, "When we are with the Messenger of God ﷺ and he reminds us of the Fire and the Garden, we can almost see them with our eyes. Then we leave his presence and return to attending to our wives and children and looking after our land, and we forget much of that." Abū Bakr said, "By God, we experience much of the same." They went to the Prophet's house, where Ḥanẓala repeated, "Ḥanẓala has become a hypocrite, O Messenger of God!" "*What is this about?*" the Prophet ﷺ asked. "When we are with you and you remind us of the Fire and the Garden, we can almost see them with our eyes," Ḥanẓala said, "then we leave your presence and return to interacting with our wives and children and looking after our land, and we forget much of that." The Prophet ﷺ said, "*By He in whose Hand rests my soul, were you to persist in the state you are with me and in remembrance, the angels would have shaken hands with you in your beds and in your streets.*" Then he repeated three times, "*But, O Ḥanẓala, sometimes this, sometimes that.*"[53] Here we see a Companion in his daily routine feeling an intense nostalgia for what he experiences in the Prophet's presence. The images of the Garden and the Fire are so vivid in his imagination that he can almost see them with his physical eyes. This is the first degree of certainty, the Knowledge of Certainty. The Prophet ﷺ then confirms that this activity of the imagination is the precursor to the Vision of Certainty, then to the Truth of Certainty, when he will actually see the angels greet him and shake hands with him.

Another example of the imagination's power is given in the episode when ʿUrwa ibn al-Zubayr met ʿAbdallāh ibn ʿUmar as they circumambulated the Kaʿba. He had it in mind to ask for the hand of Ibn ʿUmar's daughter in marriage and took the opportunity to do so. When Ibn ʿUmar said nothing, ʿUrwa wondered if he had been refused and promised himself to try again at a later date. When they had both returned to Madina, ʿUrwa visited Ibn ʿUmar at his home and, after the usual greetings, the latter said, "You spoke to me as we were circumambulating, asking for my daughter's hand, but at that time we beheld God in front of our eyes, and this is what has prevented me from answering you. Now, do you still desire the same thing?" ʿUrwa replied, "I have never been more eager."[54] Here the famous Companion ʿAbdallāh ibn

ʿUmar says that he beheld God in front of his eyes, which evidently refers to his total imaginative concentration on God during an act of worship. It is to the same concentration that the Prophet ﷺ refers when he states that as we perform the ritual prayer God stands before us,[55] or that excellence is to worship God as if we were able to see Him, for if we cannot see Him, He sees us.[56]

Another example is the Prophet ﷺ saying, "*For the one whom it would please to behold the Day of Resurrection as if he actually saw it with his own eyes, let him recite:* ***When the sun shall be darkened, When the sky is split open,*** *and* ***When the sky is rent asunder***."[57] The *sūra*s that describe the cosmic event of the Hour can form vivid scenes in the imagination that render the Day of Judgement present in the mind in such a manner so as to influence thoughts, emotions and behaviour.

Anas recounted how his paternal uncle Anas ibn al-Naḍr, having missed the first battle the Prophet ﷺ fought, which was the Battle of Badr, said, "I have missed the first battle with the Prophet ﷺ. Should God permit me to witness another day with Prophet ﷺ, He shall see how I fare." He fought on the Day of Uḥud and when they were defeated, he said, "O God, I apologise to You from what those have done [meaning the Muslims] and I am innocent of what the pagans have done!" Then he marched forward, sword in hand, and coming across Saʿd ibn Muʿādh, exclaimed, "Where are you going, Saʿd? I perceive the fragrance of the Garden from the direction of Uḥud!" Then he fought until he was killed. He suffered over eighty injuries, stabs, cuts, and arrow wounds, and could only be recognised by his sister.[58] His smelling the fragrance of Paradise from the direction of Mount Uḥud can be interpreted in one of two ways: either as a product of his imagination, driving him to fight to the death to attain martyrdom, or something that he smelt physically, in which case it would be a manifestation from the World of Similitudes.

PART THREE

The World of Similitudes

The Unseen consists of those dimensions of existence that separate the material world that we know from the transcendent Divine Presence and are not perceptible by the physical senses. We know of three main kinds of living creatures populating these dimensions: the angels, the jinn and the spirits of human beings. According to the Prophet ﷺ, the angels were created from light, the jinn from fire, and human beings from clay.[59] Thus, both angels and jinn are normally invisible, unless they choose to take an apparent form in the physical world, while human beings are normally visible.

There are several species of jinn. Some jinn are believers and some are disbelievers. An evil jinn is called a *shayṭān*, a devil.[i]

We know that Prophets and men of God are, while fully awake or lightly asleep, capable of seeing the angels, either as lights or in human or subtle forms. They are also capable of seeing the spirits of departed human beings, usually in a subtle form that resembles their previous earthly appearance or less frequently in a material form.

Spirits are formless lights and intelligible entities that can only manifest in worlds other than their own by assuming a suitable form. For a spirit to be able to live in the material world it needs a body made of the same stuff that this world is made of, a physical body that can perceive its surroundings with its senses of vision, hearing, smell, touch and taste, and can interact with and influence them with its powers of motion. Only in this manner will it be able to do what is necessary to survive, engage in pleasure seeking or pain avoidance, and fulfil its function in this life. Once the spirit leaves this world for the Interme-

---

i The Arabic *shayṭān* indicates any rebellious living creature, whether human, jinn or animal. *Shayṭān* is usually translated as devil or demon. *Al-Shayṭān*, "the Devil," indicates Satan himself, known in Arabic as Iblīs.

diary World (the *Barzakh*),[i] it needs a body appropriate to that world, which will be more subtle and allow it to subsist there until the Day of Resurrection. At that time it will acquire yet another body suitable for the events of the Resurrection and the Last Judgement. Finally, it will have the body suitable for either Paradise or Hell, as the case may be.

---

i The word *Barzakh* means a barrier that separates two different domains. It belongs to neither, but possesses sufficient resemblance to both to form an intermediary area that both separates and connects them. In the present context, it is used to designate two interconnected realities. Firstly, the realm where spirits abide between the time they die and the time they are resurrected, which is the subtle dimension that is neither of this world, nor yet of the Hereafter. Secondly, the domain of subtle forms that separates the physical from the spiritual dimensions.

I

Witnessing the Angels

Angels exist in the Spiritual World as formless entities, for light as such has no form. But when they descend to the world of subtle images or the seven heavens of the *Malakūt*,[i] they assume the form suitable for life at each level, as explained above. These are the forms described by the Qur'ān and by those who have witnessed the angels as immense, possessing numerous wings, countless eyes, and other such unimaginable attributes. When they appear in the material world they appear in human form and can be seen, heard and touched. These human forms can move about in this world, interact with other material forms and thus accomplish tasks.

We know that Gabriel often appeared in the form of the Prophet's Companion Diḥya al-Kalbī, and sometimes in the form of a stranger in white clothes, as described by 'Umar. Sometimes he came walking, sometimes riding a mare, at other times a mule. 'Ā'isha said that the very first experience the Prophet ﷺ had with Divine revelation was the true dream-vision, which always came true in as clear and sharp a manner as the break of dawn. Thereafter he took to retreating to the Cave of Ḥirā' for many nights at a time, returning to Khadīja's house for provisions before going back. Then the angel came to him in the Cave of Ḥirā' saying, "Recite!"[ii] He ﷺ answered, "I am no reciter!" So the angel embraced him, squeezing him against his chest to exhaustion, then he released him, saying, "Recite!" Again he ﷺ answered, "I am no reciter!" Once more, the angel embraced and squeezed him to

---

i The word *Malakūt* is used in the Qur'ān to designate the invisible dimensions in their entirety. However, it is also often used by scholars to designate the dimension of subtle forms.

ii Or "*Iqra'*!" This word is an imperative which means both read and recite, for the two are so inextricably linked in Arabic that a blind reciter of the Qur'ān would still be called a *qāri'*, a reader.

exhaustion, then released him, saying, "Recite!" After the third time, the angel recited, ***Recite in the name of your Lord who has created, created man from a blood clot. Recite! And your Lord is the Most Generous.***[60] The Prophet ﷺ hastened back home trembling, crying to Khadīja, "Cover me, cover me!" She wrapped him in a cloak until his distress abated. Later on, as the Companion Jābir recounted, the angel appeared again after a long absence, but this time in his tremendous *Malakūtī* form, sitting on a chair filling the entire horizon up to the sky, yet recognisable by the Prophet ﷺ as the same angel he had seen in the cave. The Prophet ﷺ described the event thus, "The angel did not come to me for a time, then one day as I was walking I heard a sound from the sky. I raised my eyes and there was the same angel that had come to me in Ḥirā', sitting on a chair that filled the space between heaven and earth."[61] Again, the vision affected him so much that he rushed home, saying, "Cover me, cover me!"[62]

These accounts involve two distinct episodes. In the first, the angel appears in physical form and is able to embrace and squeeze the Prophet ﷺ. In the second, he appears in an immense subtle form that fills the entire horizon. Thus, there are two main modes for the angel to manifest in the waking state, the human and the subtle forms.

On subsequent occasions when Gabriel appeared to the Prophet ﷺ in human form, the Companions were also sometimes able to see him, and sometimes only the Prophet ﷺ could. Other angels also appear in various forms both to the Prophets and to other mortals. In what follows we shall devote a section to each mode of manifestation.

GABRIEL APPEARING IN HIS SUBTLE FORM

In the aforementioned account of Jābir, we have a description of the Prophet's first waking vision of the tremendous subtle form of Gabriel. According to Ibn Masʿūd, the Prophet ﷺ saw him again in his subtle form on the Night of the Ascension, and described him as having six hundred wings.[63]

THE APPEARANCE OF OTHER ANGELS TO THE PROPHET ﷺ IN THEIR SUBTLE FORMS

The Prophet ﷺ also recounted how he had once offered Islām to an Arab chieftain who had declined to accept it. Sadly walking in the area outside Makka known as Qarn al-Tha'ālib, he felt a cloud come over him. Looking up, he saw Gabriel in the cloud, speaking to him, saying that God had heard what had just happened and had sent the Angel of the Mountains to him with orders to do as he bade. The Angel of the Mountains greeted him with *salām*, then said, "O Muḥammad, if you wish, I shall crush them between the two mountains of al-Akhshabayn." The Prophet ﷺ answered, "*Rather, I hope that God will bring out of their loins those who will worship God alone and associate no others with Him.*"[64]

The Prophet ﷺ also saw Seraphiel (Isrāfīl). Ibn 'Abbās narrates that once the Prophet ﷺ was speaking to Gabriel when the horizon was split open and Gabriel began to sway and huddle up closer to the ground. An angel appeared before the Prophet ﷺ and said to him, "O Muḥammad, God wishes you to choose between a Prophet who is a slave and a Prophet who is a king." Gabriel signalled to him with his hand to humble himself, so he answered, "*A Prophet who is a slave.*" The angel ascended back to Heaven; and upon asking Gabriel about his identity, the Prophet ﷺ was told that he was Seraphiel. He then added that he thought he had come down because it was the Hour and that was why he had shown such fear.[65]

On the Day of Uḥud, after Ḥanẓala was killed, the Prophet ﷺ informed his Companions that he had seen the angels washing him in the air. He was newly-wed, so when they returned to Madina they asked his bride and she told them that they had slept together just before he had been summoned to battle. He thus had had no time to bathe.[66] When the Prophet ﷺ says he has seen the martyr being washed by angels in the air, we must understand what he means is that he saw the scene happening in the subtle dimension of the Intermediary World, which we know was unveiled to him at all times. What attracted his attention to this particular scene is that the bodies of martyrs are considered pure, and therefore require no ritual washing before burial. They are normally buried in their blood-stained clothes, unwashed. The fact that the angels were washing him was therefore unusual and required an explanation. We are only told that the angels were washing the martyr in the air, which leads us to conclude that they were in their subtle forms.

ANGELS SEEN BY OTHERS IN THEIR SUBTLE FORMS

As for people who are not Prophets witnessing the angels in their subtle forms, we are told that Khadīja's servant Maysara, who accompanied the Prophet ﷺ to Syria on one of his trading trips, saw two angels shading the Prophet ﷺ from the sun when it was high and the weather had become hot. They were also seen by one of the Christian monks in the Syrian Desert near Buṣrā, but by no one else.[67]

We were also told that two of the Prophet's Companions, Salmān and Abū Hurayra, stated that Pharaoh's wife was being tortured in the sun and, whenever her torturers drew away from her, the angels shaded her with their wings, and she could see her mansion in the Garden.[68]

GABRIEL APPEARING IN A HUMAN FORM SEEN ONLY BY THE PROPHET ﷺ

The Prophet ﷺ once said to his wife, "*O ʿĀ'isha, this is Gabriel giving you his greetings of peace (salām).*" She said, "And upon him be peace and the mercy of God and His blessings. You see what I do not."[69] On this occasion only the Prophet ﷺ was able to see and hear the angel. A similar occasion was reported by Ibn ʿAbbās, who said that on the Day of Badr the Prophet ﷺ said that he saw Gabriel on his horse, attired for war.

GABRIEL SEEN BY OTHERS IN A HUMAN FORM

The Qur'ān says, ***Mention in the Book Mary as she withdrew from her people to an eastern place. She took a screen apart from them. We sent to her Our Spirit that appeared to her as a fair human being.***[70] Thus did Gabriel appear in human form to Mary. She did not recognise him for what he was and was frightened. He had to inform her of his identity and mission.

Before Mary, Gabriel had appeared to Hagar. Recounting how Abraham had left his wife Hagar (Hājar) and her baby son Ishmael (Ismāʿīl) in the desert in Makka, the Prophet ﷺ said that Hagar had heard a voice, even though there was no one around to be seen. She exclaimed, "I hear your voice, help me if there is any good in you!" At this, Gabriel appeared to her and she followed him to a spot where he struck the sand with his heel, making water gush out of the ground where the Well of Zamzam was later to be dug.[71] Even before that, an angel had been sent to her in the wilderness of the Negev, near Beersheba, when, pregnant with Ishmael, she had fled in distress. As she rested near a well, the angel comforted her, informing her that God had heard her cries of distress and wished her to receive the good news that the child in her womb would be blessed with ***Such abundant progeny that it shall not be numbered for multitude.***[72]

An episode involving the appearance of the angel in a physical form that was not only seen by the Prophet ﷺ, but by all his Companions, was recounted by ʿUmar. It occurred in Madina when the Prophet ﷺ was sitting with his Companions in the Prophetic Mosque. A man appeared whose clothes were very white, whose hair was very black, and upon whom, despite being a stranger, no sign of travelling could be seen. He sat down on the ground facing the Prophet ﷺ so that their knees touched, and asked him about *Islām*, *Īmān*, and *Iḥsān*, and then about the signs of the Hour. Having received his answer, he departed and the Prophet ﷺ informed them that he was Gabriel, who had come to teach them their religion.[73]

Gabriel was again seen by all the Companions soon after the Prophet ﷺ had returned home after the end of the Siege of the Trench. Gabriel came to the Prophet ﷺ with dust on his face and, standing at his door, requested him not to take off his armour, but to march immediately to the fortifications of the Jewish tribe of Banī Qurayẓa. They had betrayed the Prophet ﷺ to his enemies during the siege and he was to fight them. As he rode through the quarters of the Banī Ghanm of the Anṣār, immediately to the south of the mosque, the Prophet ﷺ asked them, "*Have you seen anyone passing by?*" They replied, "Yes, Diḥya al-Kalbī has passed by."[74] For on that day Gabriel had taken the form of Diḥya, as he often did. Anas, the young servant of the Prophet ﷺ, said, "I can still see the dust rising in the Banī Ghanm Alley from the procession of Gabriel, when the Messenger of God ﷺ marched to the Banī Qurayẓa."[75]

In addition, another Companion, Ḥāritha ibn al-Nuʿmān, once walked by the Prophet ﷺ and noticed him sitting with Gabriel. He greeted them with *salām* as he passed by. On his way back the Prophet ﷺ stopped and asked him, "*Did you see who was with me?*" He answered, "Yes." He said, "*That was Gabriel and he returned your greeting.*"[76]

On a further occasion, a man of the Anṣār once saw the Prophet ﷺ standing with another man. Wishing to greet the Prophet ﷺ, he sat down waiting. A long while afterwards the man departed and, having greeted the Prophet ﷺ, the man of the Anṣār remarked, "O Messenger of God, you stood so long with that man that I worried about you standing so long." "*Do you know who that was?*" the Prophet ﷺ asked him. "No," he answered. So he said, "*That was Gabriel recommending my neighbours to me so insistently that I thought he would allow them to inherit.*"[77] On all the above occasions the Companions were able to see Gabriel, but thought he was a human being, for only the Prophet ﷺ was able to perceive his identity.

ʿĀ'isha said, "I saw Gabriel – may blessings and peace be upon him – standing in this room of mine, while the Messenger of God ﷺ spoke to him. When he had done I asked, "O Messenger of God, who was that?" "*Who did he look like?*" he asked, and I said, "Diḥya al-Kalbī." He said, "*You have witnessed much good. That was Gabriel – peace be upon him.*" Soon afterwards he said, "*ʿĀ'isha, this is Gabriel greeting you with peace.*" I answered, "And may peace be upon him. May God reward our guest on our behalf."[78]

On other occasions, some of the Companions saw a man dressed in white having an intimate conversation with the Prophet ﷺ. They subsequently asked him who that was and he told them it had been Gabriel, who had been strongly enjoining the good treatment of neighbours; and had they given him their greetings of peace, he would have greeted them back.[79]

OTHER ANGELS APPEARING IN A HUMAN FORM SEEN ONLY BY THE PROPHET ﷺ

There was an occasion when the Prophet ﷺ informed his Companions who had seen nothing that he had noticed that the two guardian angels of a certain man were perplexed, unable to decide how to record his praises. The man had said, "O Lord, Yours is all praise and thanks, as is worthy of the majesty of Your Countenance and the immensity of Your sovereignty." They asked their Lord what they should do and were told to record his words as they had heard them, so that He might reward him Himself when they meet.[80]

Sometimes only the voice of the angel was heard. For instance, Ḥudhayfa ibn al-Yamān told the Prophet ﷺ that while he was praying he had heard a voice praising God and asking for His forgiveness and favours. The Prophet ﷺ said that an angel had come to teach him how to praise and thank his Lord.[81]

Saʿd ibn Muʿādh was wounded during the Siege of the Trench, died following the Siege of Banī Qurayẓa,[i] and was carried to the Baqīʿ Cemetery. Some of the Hypocrites remarked that he had been surprisingly light to carry despite being a rather corpulent man. The Prophet ﷺ told them that the angels had helped to carry him.[82]

Furthermore, the Prophet ﷺ described what he saw on Fridays, saying, "*When Friday comes, angels stand at the doors of the mosques, recording the order in which people enter, the first ones first. Once the imām sits on the pulpit, they fold up their records and enter to listen to the remembrance.*"[83] He also described what he saw of the Unseen at sunrise and sunset, saying, "*Never does the sun rise without two angels at its sides – heard by all on earth save the two Weighty Ones* [human beings and jinn] *– crying, 'O humans, come to your Lord! That which is little but sufficient is better than that which is plentiful but distracting.' And never does the sun set without two angels at its sides crying, 'O God, he who spends, repay him; but he who withholds, ruin him.'*"[84]

On more than one occasion, the Prophet ﷺ informed his Compan-

---

i A Companion of the Prophet ﷺ. He was the chief of the Aws Tribe of the Anṣār and died of an arrow wound received during the Siege of the Trench in the third year of the Hijra.

ions that he had seen the angels competing with one another in recording and lifting up to the Divine Presence the praises of those who were attending congregational prayers in the mosque and praised their Lord in words that they had improvised.[85] He also informed them that he had seen the angels wearing loincloths wrapped around their waists to a particular length, and he instructed them to follow suit.[86] In addition, he saw the angels on the Day of Badr. He said, "*I see that the angels have marked their helmets, so mark yours with wool.*"[87] As mentioned before, on the Day of Uḥud, he saw the angels washing some of the martyrs; and following the siege of the Banī Qurayẓa, he saw them carrying the bier of Saʿd ibn Muʿādh.[88]

ANGELS SEEN BY OTHERS IN A HUMAN FORM

According to Ubayy ibn Kaʿb, God ordered the Prophet David – may peace be upon him – to build him a House. David asked where he was to build it and was told to do so where he would see an angel standing, sword drawn. He saw him on the Rock of Jerusalem.[89]

We know from the Qur'ān that it is possible for angels to appear in human form and hide their inner reality so well that even a major Prophet like Abraham cannot detect it: ***Our envoys came to Abraham with glad tidings. They said, "Peace," and soon he brought a roasted calf; but when he saw their hands not reaching towards it, he became suspicious and apprehensive. They said, "Fear not! We have been sent to the people of Lot."***[90] So here we see Abraham, one of the greatest of the Divine Messengers, not recognizing his guests for who they were and worrying about their not touching his food, which in Semitic custom means they are rejecting his hospitality because they intend him some harm. The same group of angels then travelled to Sodom, headed for Lot's house and knocked on his door. He also was unable to recognise them for who they were until they informed him. They were seen and thought to be human beings by everyone else, believers and pagans alike.[91]

Among the stories that the Prophet ﷺ told his Companions was one that clearly demonstrates that ordinary people can very well see the angels and converse with them when they appear in human form. He said that as a man was on his way to visit a fellow believer in another village, God sent an angel to meet him on the road. When they met, the angel questioned him to ascertain that there was no worldly reason for the visit and that he simply loved his fellow believer for the sake of God. The angel then declared, "I am God's messenger to you to inform you that God loves you just as you love this man for His sake."[92]

The likelihood of seeing the angels obviously increases the more the spiritual stature of a person increases, as may be understood from the aforementioned *ḥadīth* of Ḥanẓala al-Usaydī complaining to the Prophet ﷺ of hypocrisy due to failing to maintain the heightened awareness of the Hereafter when he returned from the Prophet's gathering to his normal family life; so the Prophet ﷺ told him that had they, meaning him and the other Companions, been able to maintain themselves in the state they had in his presence, then the angels would have shaken hands with them in their bedrooms and in the streets.[93]

Once another Companion of the Prophet ﷺ was travelling on his own through the wilderness, when a masked brigand blocked his path, threatening to kill him. In vain did he plead with him to take his money and spare his life, but the brigand retorted that what he really wanted was his life. In despair, he asked him to permit him to pray four *rakʿa*s, to which the brigand agreed. He prayed the four *rakʿa*s, then followed his prayer with an ardent supplication to God, beseeching Him by His names to save him. Then, a rider appeared armed with a spear. As soon as the brigand saw him, he charged the rider, only to be speared to death. The Companion asked his saviour who he was and was told he was an angel from the Fourth Heaven, where his supplications had been heard; and that he had asked God to allow him to be the one to intervene.[94]

The Qur'ān states that the angels descend with reassurance and good news upon those who had been upright in this world: ***Those who have said, "Our Lord is God," then were upright, upon them angels will descend, [saying], "Fear not, neither grieve, and rejoice with the Garden you have been promised."***[95] According to Mujāhid, this refers to the time of death when the angels come to the believers to reassure them that neither should they fear what is about to happen nor grieve for the families they are leaving behind. They also make them rejoice with the good news that they are about to enter the Garden that they had been promised.

Ibn ʿAbbās reports that he had heard from a man of the Banī Ghifār that he had been there on the Day of Badr together with one of his cousins, both being pagans at the time. They were on the ridge of a hill, watching the battle, waiting to loot the defeated army. Then they saw a cloud appear and, as it was passing over their heads, they heard horses neighing and the voice of one of the riders saying, "Forward, Ḥayzūm!" They were both so frightened that one of them died, while the other lived to recount the episode.[96] This was seen and heard by pagans. As for what the Prophet's Companions witnessed, we have numerous testimonies among which are the following.

Imām ʿAlī recounted how, as he was drawing water from the basin at Badr, a mighty wind swept over them, then another, then a third. The first was Gabriel accompanied by a thousand angels in support of the Prophet ﷺ. The second was Michael, accompanied by another thousand angels, in aid of Abū Bakr, who was on the Prophet's right. The third was Seraphiel, accompanied by yet another thousand angels, to succour ʿAlī, who was on the Prophet's left.[97] A similar account was given by Saʿd ibn Abī Waqqāṣ concerning the Day of Uḥud. He said, "I saw the Messenger of God ﷺ on the Day of Uḥud, with two men fighting strenuously at his side, protecting him, dressed in white, whom I had never seen before or since."[98] In other versions, they were said to have been Gabriel and Michael. However, it was not only the great archangels that were seen, but also their accompanying troops. Ibn ʿAbbās stated that on the Day of Badr the angels took the forms of men that were known to the Muslims, so as to encourage them.[99]

As for later generations, it is reported that Fuḍāla ibn Dīnār said, "When Muḥammad ibn Wāsiʿ[i] was laid down before he died he was heard saying, 'Welcome to the angels of my Lord. There is neither ability nor strength save by God!' I then smelled a perfume unlike anything I had ever smelled before. Soon he lifted his gaze up and died."[100]

---

[i] Fuḍāla ibn Dīnār al-Shaḥḥām and Muḥammad ibn Wāsiʿ al-Azdī were scholars, *ḥadīth* transmitters and saints of the third generation, that of the Followers of the Followers.

Once during the pilgrimage, Sufyān al-Thawrī noticed a young man ceaselessly reciting invocations of blessings upon the Prophet ﷺ.[i] He pointed out to him that it would be more appropriate in this situation to address praises and prayers to God. He replied that he once had a brother whose face turned black when he died, which caused him much distress. Then he saw a man enter whose face was like a radiant lamp. As soon as this man passed his hand over his brother's face, its darkness disappeared and it became like the moon. Overjoyed, he asked the stranger for his name and was told, "I am an angel responsible for looking after those who invoked blessings on the Prophet ﷺ. Your brother used to invoke blessings on the Prophet ﷺ in abundance. He had gone through a bad time and been punished with the blackening of his face. Then, by the blessings of his invocations of blessings on the Prophet ﷺ, God saved him and removed that from him, dressing him as you see."[101] In this story the darkening of the dead man's face probably pertains to the World of Similitude and in all likelihood it would not have been perceived by everyone there. Similarly, not everyone would have seen the angel nor the effect of his action on the dead man's face.

Ibrāhīm ibn Adham, one of the earliest Sufis who flourished in the third century of the Hijra, recounted how he had once spent the night near the Rock of Jerusalem.[ii] When part of the night had gone by, two angels descended, one saying to the other, "Who is this man there?" "Ibrāhīm ibn Adham," was the answer. The first angel asked again, "He whose degree with God has diminished?" "Why was that?" the second asked and the first answered, "Because when in Baṣra buying dates, a date belonging to the merchant dropped among his dates and he did not give it back." Upon witnessing this, Ibrāhīm returned to Baṣra, bought dates from the same man, dropped one back, and retraced his steps back to Jerusalem. He once more spent the night at the same spot and again two angels descended, one saying to the other, "Who is this

i Sufyān al-Thawrī was one of the most famous scholars and transmitters of *ḥadīth* among the second generation, that of the Followers. He lived in Kufa, became renowned for his detachment from the world and his sanctity, and died in 161 AH.

ii The rock in question is the one from which the Prophet ﷺ began his Ascension. It now lies under the Dome of the Rock in Jerusalem, the same rock upon which David saw the angel standing sword in hand.

man there?" The other again answered, "Ibrāhīm ibn Adham." He said, "He whose degree God has restored and then raised some more?"[102]

Ibn Hubayra[i] is reported to have said that once, as he was invoking blessings on the Prophet ﷺ with his eyes closed, he saw someone through his eyelids writing down his invocations in black ink on a parchment, adding that he could clearly distinguish the letters on the parchment. He opened his eyes to see him, and just managed to catch a glimpse of him departing in his white clothes.[103]

WITNESSING THE ANGEL OF DEATH

We know that when the Angel of Death came to the Prophets, usually in the form of a man, they saw him, sometimes recognizing him at first sight, and sometimes not. For instance, when the time had come for Adam to die, the Angel of Death came, was immediately recognised by him, and they had a conversation.[104] But when he came to David (Dāwūd) in the form of a man whom he saw standing inside his apartments, he did not recognise him, and asked him sharply who he was. He replied, "I am the one who fears not the kings and who is resisted by nothing." "Then by God," said David, "you are the Angel of Death! Welcome then to the command of God."[105] As for Enoch, known to us as Idrīs, he was said by the Prophet ﷺ to be a friend of the Angel of Death.[106]

Suddī[ii] said that when God decided to choose Abraham to make him His friend, the Angel of Death requested permission to be the one to announce the good news to him. Permission granted, he entered the house and, like David would be after him, Abraham was taken aback by the sudden appearance of this stranger in his home. He asked him sharply, "Who permitted you to enter this house?" When he replied, "The Lord of this house," Abraham recognised him for whom he was

---

i Abu'l-Muẓaffar Yaḥyā ibn Hubayra was a famous Abbasid prime minister who was known for his virtuous character, generosity and wisdom. He was a scholar of the religious sciences and an expert on *ḥadīth*, and also a man of letters. He died in Baghdad in 560 AH.

ii Ismāʿīl ibn ʿAbd al-Raḥmān al-Suddī was a Qurayshī Follower from Kufa who was a scholar and an authority on Qur'ānic exegesis. He died in 127 AH.

and said, "You have spoken truly." Having received the good news, Abraham asked the angel to show him the manner in which he seized the souls of the disbelievers. The angel warned him that he would not be able to bear it. However, Abraham insisted, so the angel asked him to look the other way for a moment. When he looked back, he saw a black man from whose mouth and ears came flames. Abraham fainted at the sight. When he came to, he asked to be shown the form in which he seized the lives of the believers and was shown a kind-faced, fragrant young man dressed in white.[107]

Prophet Solomon – may peace be upon him - is also known to have been a friend of the Angel of Death.[108]

On one of the occasions that the Prophet ﷺ saw the Angel of Death, who stood near the head of a man of the Helpers, he said to him, "*O Angel of Death! Be gentle on my Companion, for he is a believer.*" The angel replied, "Be of good cheer and be well pleased, for I am gentle with all believers."[109]

During his terminal illness he was visited repeatedly by Gabriel. One day he said to him, "O Muḥammad, the Angel of Death is here, asking permission to enter. He has never asked a human being's permission before and will never ask a human being's permission after you." He answered, "*Permit him.*" The angel approached until he stood before him, then said, "O Muḥammad, God – August and Majestic is He – has sent me to you, commanding me to obey your bidding. If you bid me to seize your soul, then I shall; if you are averse to that I shall leave it be." The Prophet ﷺ asked, "*Would you, Angel of Death?*" He replied, "Yes, I have been commanded to obey your bidding." At this point Gabriel said, "God desires to meet you." So the Prophet ﷺ said, "*Do your bidding, then.*"[110]

Near the end of his life, the Companion ʿAbd al-Raḥmān ibn ʿAwf was once seen to lose consciousness. When he came round, he said, "Two rude, harsh angels came for me, saying, 'Come, for we shall take you to be judged before the August, the Trustworthy!' They were halted by two gentler angels who asked them where they were taking me, to which they answered that they were taking me to be judged before the August, the Trustworthy. They said, 'Leave him be, for he is one for whom happiness has been decreed even when he was in his mother's womb.'" 'Abd al-Raḥmān lived a month after this episode.[111] This was not a dream, but an inner vision experienced by a man who was outwardly thought to be unconscious. Experiences of this kind are frequently reported by ordinary people who have had near death experiences, those who have recovered from a coma, and spiritual people who lose consciousness under the effect of the experience.

The Prophet ﷺ once said to 'Ā'isha, "*When the believer sees the angels – meaning after his death – they ask him, 'Shall we return you to the world?' He answers, 'To the abode of anxieties and sorrows?' before requesting, 'Advance me to meet God!' As for the disbeliever, when asked if they should return him, he answers, 'My Lord, send me back, so that I may make good what I have neglected.'*"[112]

A short while before he died, Khayr al-Nassāj,[i] one of the great early Sufis, lost consciousness. It was time for the Sunset Prayer. He came to, opened his eyes, looked insistently towards one side of the house, and was heard saying, "Stop, may God grant you well-being! You are but a slave under orders and I am but a slave under orders. What you have been ordered to do, you cannot miss; but what I have been ordered to do, I can." He then asked for water, made his ablutions, prayed, then laid down, closed his eyes, uttered the Two Testimonies, and passed away.[113]

I was told by my friend Muḥammad Yūsuf that his teacher Shaykh Ibrāhīm Ḥilmī al-Qādirī of Alexandria had died in 1970 CE in the month of Ramaḍān. He had returned to the mosque with a group of disciples for the *'ishā'* and *tarāwīḥ* prayers, having broken the fast together. As soon as he reached the doorstep of the mosque, he stopped, leaning on his cane, lowered his head down, and was heard repeating three times, "Welcome and greetings!" The disciples behind him were puzzled, for they had not left his side and there was no reason for him to greet them again. He entered the mosque and led the prayers as usual. In the twelfth *rak'a* of the *tarāwīḥ* prayers he went into prostration and never sat up again. Those behind him waited, hoping to see

---

i Khayr al-Nassāj was one of the earlier generations of Sufi masters who appeared in the fourth century of the Hijra in Iraq and Iran. He died in 322 AH.

him rise, but, when it became obvious that something was amiss, the man immediately behind him hesitantly touched his heel, eliciting no response. The Shaykh had passed away in prostration and the invisible person he had been greeting as he entered had been none other than the Angel of Death.

WITNESSING THE ANGELS IN THE FORM OF BIRDS

Saʿīd ibn Jubayr, Maymūn ibn Mihrān,[i] and other Followers said they attended the funeral of ʿAbdallāh ibn ʿAbbās at Ṭā'if. When the body was placed on the ground in preparation for the prayer, a white bird came flying down, landed on the shrouds, and then penetrated into them. They searched for it but found nothing. After the burial, although no speaker was seen, a voice was heard saying, ***O soul at peace, return to your Lord, well pleased and well pleasing! Enter among My servants and enter My Garden!***[114]

Shaykh Muḥammad al-Ḥazīn al-Firsāfī of Kurdistan[ii] informed his students that the angels attend the funeral of certain saints in the form of beautiful birds. When he died and his bier was being carried to his grave, extraordinarily beautiful birds hovered over the procession and the funeral prayer, departing only after he had been lowered into his grave.[115]

THE ANGELS AS LIGHTS (THE *SAKĪNA*)

The angels may appear as lights, in which case they are called the *Sakīna*. Usayd ibn Ḥuḍayr recounted that one night he was reading the Qur'ān in his stable, with his mare tied up not far from him, when she suddenly became restless. He stopped reciting and she calmed down, but when he resumed his recitation she became restless again. He stopped again and again she calmed down. A third time he started reciting and

---

i Both Saʿīd ibn Jubayr, who was executed by Ḥajjāj in 95 AH, and Maymūn ibn Mihrān, who died in 117 AH, were illustrious Followers, scholars, transmitters of *ḥadīth* and men of great spirituality.

ii Shaykh Muḥammad al-Ḥazīn al-Firsāfī was a great Kurdistani scholar and spiritual master. He lived in the small town of Firsāf, where he died in 1304 AH.

when she became agitated he stopped altogether fearing that his infant son Yaḥyā who was sleeping on the ground nearby might be trampled. He looked up and saw something that he likened to a cloud full of lamps. When he recounted this to the Prophet ﷺ in the morning he was told that these were the angels approaching at the sound of the Qur'ān and that had he not stopped his recitation they would have stayed with him until morning for all to see.[116]

The unseen happenings in Qur'ān gatherings were thus described by the Prophet ﷺ: "*Never shall people gather in a house of God to recite the Book of God and study it without the* Sakīna *descending upon them, mercy enveloping them, the angels surrounding them, and God mentioning them to those in His presence.*"[117]

THE NIGHT OF DESTINY (*LAYLAT AL-QADR*)

Shaykh Ibn ʿAṭā'illāh al-Iskandarī[i] wrote in *Laṭā'if al-Minan* that he was with Shaykh Makīn al-Dīn al-Asmar[ii] in the Western Mosque of Alexandria during one of the last ten nights in Ramaḍān, specifically the night of the twenty-sixth. Shaykh Makīn al-Dīn said, "I can now see the angels ascending and descending, gathering and preparing. Have you seen how the family of the bride begins to prepare the night before? This is how I see them." The next night, the night of the twenty-seventh, was also the night before Friday, and he said, "I see the angels now carrying plates of light, each plate as big as the minaret of the mosque, some a little bigger, some a little smaller. This is the Night of Destiny."[118] Here we have a man of God witnessing the angels preparing for the greatest night of the year in the Muslim calendar, the Night of Destiny, mentioned in the Qur'ān in a *sūra* specially devoted to it and

---

i Shaykh Ibn ʿAṭā'illah al-Iskandarī was the third master of the Shādhilī order. He taught at the Azhar University and wrote numerous books of Sufism, a number of which became famous and are still taught to this day. He died in Cairo in 709 AH and was buried at the foot of the Muqaṭṭam Hill.

ii Shaykh Makīn al-Dīn al-Asmar came to Egypt from Abyssinia to become a disciple of Shaykh Abu'l-Ḥasan al-Shādhilī. He died in Alexandria and was buried near the mosque and tomb of Shaykh al-Shādhilī's successor, Shaykh Abu'l-ʿAbbās al-Mursī.

said by the Prophet ﷺ to occur most frequently in the last ten nights of Ramaḍān and to be more likely to fall in the odd nights.

THE *SAKĪNA* APPEARING IN THE FORM OF A WIND

The Prophet ﷺ said that the *Sakīna* was a whirling wind.[119] And ʿAlī said that when God commanded Abraham to build a House for Him on earth, He sent him the *Sakīna,* which is a swift whirling wind with a head. Abraham then followed it until it curled itself up like a snake at the location of the House'.[120]

A HIGHER REALITY

2
Witnessing the Spirits in the Intermediary World

Similar to the angels who appear in human form in the material dimension, the spirits of the Prophets of old are capable of donning a physical body to appear in this world in physical form. They can also appear as subtle forms that will then not be visible to everyone, nor be able to interact with the physical environment. As for those Prophets who have not died in the usual manner, but who have been lifted up to the heavens, such as Jesus, Enoch and Elijah (Ilyās), their bodies acquire more and more subtlety as they ascend to enable them to penetrate the subtle dimensions. On the other hand, when they retrace their steps back to earth they acquire more and more density as they descend, until they appear in a fully materialised form similar to other humans.

THE PROPHET ﷺ SEEING THE SPIRITS OF OTHER PROPHETS

On the night of his Ascension, when fully awake, the Prophet ﷺ met most, if not all, of the previous Prophets: those who had passed away in this world and were living the life of the spirits in the Intermediary World, and those who had been lifted up to the subtle dimension, as mentioned above. He saw them clearly and was later able to describe them. He described Moses as tall, having tanned skin and coarse hair, and Jesus as of medium build, with a reddish-white complexion and soft hair.[121] He recounted how in the course of that journey he had seen Moses standing up in prayer in his grave at the red hill.[122] He also saw the great angel Mālik, guardian of Hell, and the Dajjāl, who is yet to appear in this world at the end of time. According to Ibn ʿAbbās, who specifically stated that it had been a waking vision and not a dream, the Prophet ﷺ had been shown the Dajjāl in his actual form.[123]

The Prophet ﷺ also informed his Companions that one of the merits of the Mosque of al-Khayf in Minā was that seventy Prophets had prayed in it,[i] including Moses, who he had seen riding a camel down the valley uttering the *talbiya*,[124] and that he had also seen him dressed in two *iḥrām* cloths.[125]

On another occasion, he asked his Companions, "*What valley is this?*" They answered, "Wādī al-Azraq."[ii] He ﷺ said, "*It is as if I am looking at Moses – peace be upon him – coming down the pass, raising his voice with the* talbiya." Then they came to the Pass of Harshā[iii] and he ﷺ said, "*Which pass is this?*" They answered, "The Pass of Harshā." He ﷺ said, "*It is as if I am looking at Yūnus, son of Mattā[iv] – peace be upon him – on a red she-camel, wearing a woollen cloak, with a fibre bridle for his camel, repeating the* talbiya."[126] In such contexts, the expression "*it is as if I am looking*" usually indicates that the vision pertains to the World of Similitudes.

BELIEVERS SEEING THE SPIRITS OF THE PROPHETS

Over the centuries, reports have abounded of the Prophet ﷺ himself being seen by members of his community who are fully awake, starting with the Companions and the Followers, then the innumerable Sufi masters who have reported seeing the Prophet ﷺ in a waking state. This vision is sometimes that of a subtle image and less frequently that of a fully materialised human being. One of them, Shaykh Jalāl al-Dīn al-Suyūṭī, said, "I saw the Prophet ﷺ in a waking state and he addressed me as 'Shaykh al-Ḥadīth'. I asked him, 'Am I one of the people of the Garden?' he answered, '*Yes.*'" The Shaykh went on asking, "Without prior punishment?" and was answered, "*This shall be granted to you.*" He then wrote a book devoted to this subject, entitled *Tanwīr al-ḥalak*

---

i Minā is a valley between Makka and 'Arafāt where the pilgrims spend the night before 'Arafāt and return afterwards for the three or four days of the 'Īd or Feast. The Mosque of al-Khayf in Minā is ancient.

ii Wādī al-Azraq is a valley in the Ḥijāz Desert to the north of Makka.

iii The Harshā Pass is on the old caravan route in the Ḥijāz, lying midway between Makka and Madina.

iv This is the biblical Prophet Jonah.

fī imkān ru'yat al-Nabī wa'l-malak.[i] Once he was asked, "How many times did you see the Prophet ﷺ in the waking state?" Imām Suyūṭī answered, "More than seventy times."[127]

Another man of God, Shaykh Ibrāhīm al-Matbūlī, one of the greatest saints of the ninth century of the Hijra, had no spiritual master other than the Prophet ﷺ. He is reported by Imām Shaʿrānī to have been used to seeing the Prophet ﷺ in his youth, most frequently in dream-visions. But each time he informed his mother, she would say, "My son, a man is he who meets the Prophet ﷺ when awake." When eventually he reported to her that he had finally met him fully awake, she said, "Now you have joined the rank of men!"[128]

Shaykh Nūr al-Dīn al-Shūnī, a great Azhar teacher of the tenth century of the Hijra, said that he would not declare that he had designated Shaykh Shihāb al-Dīn al-Bulqīnī as his successor and handed him the direction of his teaching circle until he had discussed the matter with the Prophet ﷺ. Shaykh al-Shūnī used to hold sessions of invocations of blessings on the Prophet ﷺ at the Azhar Mosque. He started at sunset on Thursday and continued uninterruptedly until the call for the Friday prayer. When in the course of the session he stood up, his students knew that he was witnessing the Prophet ﷺ and they all rose to their feet with him. Shaykh al-Bulqīnī himself eventually came to be known as one of those who had frequent meetings with the Prophet ﷺ in a waking state. He was also known for seeing the jinn and conversing with them.[129]

Shaykh Sulaymān al-Khuḍayrī recounted to Imām Shaʿrānī that once, as he was sitting at the door of the funerary mosque of Imām Shāfiʿī, he saw a group of people approaching from the side of the hill dressed in white with a cloud of light over their heads. When they drew close he recognised the Prophet ﷺ and his Companions. He rose to him and kissed his hand. They then informed him where they were heading.[130]

Other men of God explicitly said to have met the Prophet ﷺ in their waking state include *Sayyid* Aḥmad ibn Idrīs,[131] Shaykh ʿAbd al-ʿAzīz

---

i Illuminating the Shadows with the Possibility of Seeing the Prophet and the Angels.

al-Dabbāgh, Imām ʿAbdallāh al-Ḥaddād and others.

Shaykh ʿAbd al-Raḥmān ibn ʿAlī al-Khiyārī of Madina was known to see the Prophet ﷺ in full wakefulness.[i] Once, during a teaching session when they had completed a book of *ḥadīth* and begun the closing prayers, he was seen to stand up and raise his hands as if for someone else's prayers. The students and everyone else in attendance rose to their feet, but when he stood for too long, completely absorbed, some of them left. Then he resumed his prayers and concluded the session. The students asked him what had happened, for they had never seen him do this before, he replied, "By God, I stood up only when I saw the Messenger of God ﷺ praying for us. I waited until he was finished."[132]

When the previously-mentioned Shaykh Muḥammad al-Ḥazīn al-Firsāfī of Kurdistan visited Madina, he asked one of the keepers of the Prophet's Chamber to let him so that he could visit the Prophet ﷺ from inside the chamber. This was done on rare occasions in the old days. The keeper was himself obviously a saint of no mean rank, for he later recounted to the Shaykh's son how he had entered the Chamber and asked, and received, the Prophet's permission to allow the Shaykh in. Once inside, the Shaykh greeted the Prophet ﷺ and both he and the keeper clearly heard the answer.[133]

Shaykh Fakhr al-Dīn, the son of Shaykh Muḥammad al-Firsāfī,[ii] went with a group of scholars to visit the Prophet ﷺ. He walked behind them, allowing the elders to precede him. When they entered the Prophet's Mosque a man saw them and immediately came up to him exclaiming, "O Shaykh, why do you fall behind? It is your rightful place to walk in front of the others so that the people may greet and benefit from you, and receive your knowledge and secrets!" The Shaykh rebuked him, saying, "Leave all this, O shaykh! I am not what

---

i Shaykh ʿAbd al-Raḥmān ibn ʿAlī al-Khiyārī was a *sharīf* from Madina who studied at al-Azhar University in Cairo under the great masters of his time, then emigrated to Madina in 1029 AH. by permission of the Prophet ﷺ to teach and give the Friday Sermon at the Prophet's Mosque. He was an expert in all religious sciences, especially *ḥadīth*. He died in 1056 AH.

ii Shaykh Fakhr al-Dīn al-Firsāfī was also a scholar and a spiritual successor of his father. The latter assigned him to the village of Erbin in Kurdistan where he acted as a spiritual master until his death in 1330 AH/1914 CE.

you think; I am but a servant of the scholars and my companions." The man persisted, "Why do you speak thus? By God Almighty, I saw with my own eyes that the Messenger of God ﷺ came to you, held you to his breast, and welcomed you." But the Shaykh merely rebuked him again. Having returned home to Kurdistan, the Shaykh heard some of his companions talking about this. He reprimanded them sharply and ordered them never to mention this story again.[134]

Shaykh Aḥmad Ḥijāb recounts that he was once sitting with his Shaykh, *Sayyid* Muḥammad al-Sharīf. Suddenly the Shaykh said, "Do not speak to me now, as the Prophet ﷺ has arrived." Half an hour later the Shaykh resumed his conversation with him.[135] The same *Sayyid* Muḥammad once taught him how to visit dead saints in their tombs, saying that before entering the shrine, he should ask forgiveness of God eleven times. He went on, "When you enter, if you see the saint then face him, but if you see nothing then stand wherever you wish and recite eleven times *Lā ilāha illa'llāh*, adding *Muḥammadun Rasūlu'llāh* once at the end, for the saint's spirit comes at the invocation of *Lā ilāha illa'llāh*."[136] The implication is that not only did he normally expect to see the saint's spirit whenever he visited his tomb, but he also expected others to see him.

Once in Madina, as Shaykh Muḥammad Aḥmad Riḍwān was climbing the stairs of my house to attend a gathering of brothers, he said to me, "I never enter anywhere unless I see either the Prophet or my father entering first."

Thirty years ago my late friend ʿĀṭif Rifʿat and I were standing before the house of the Lady Fāṭima al-Zahrā', the Prophet's daughter, now inside the Prophet's Chamber in his Mosque. We were busy reciting our salutations to her, her husband Imām ʿAlī and her children, when noticing us, the Wahhābī guards rebuked us in their usual rude manner, saying there was no one there to greet. As we walked away, I heard ʿĀṭif mutter, softly laughing to himself, "No one there? I saw her standing in there together with Imām Ḥasan and Imām Ḥusayn." ʿĀṭif, an Egyptian professor of medicine, was only working in Madina so that he could live there for a while. He was a practical down-to-earth physician, but also a man who recited endless invocations and had strong spiritual affiliations. Witnessing the spirits of departed men of God was to him a fairly common occurrence, but he was always very reticent to talk about it. He knew that such visions should be treated as Divine secrets and divulging them to the spiritually untrained was likely to bring about sanctions, such as to be deprived of them for a time or even permanently.

One of the architects involved in maintenance and repair work at the Prophet's Mosque, the Egyptian Ṭāriq al-Sharīf, reports that in 1406 AH he was with a group of men working on the rooftop of the mosque and they had all stopped to pray the *maghrib* Prayer, after which they had sat down to rest. He was overtaken by light somnolence and saw that he was sitting in a circle in the Prophet's presence. Someone was going around serving dates, milk and coffee. When it was his turn, he was overjoyed to hear the Prophet ﷺ say, "*Serve him, for he deserves more.*"[137]

BELIEVERS SEEING THE SPIRITS OF OTHER MEN

Ibn al-Qayyim[i] reports that once when Muṭarrif[ii] reached the graveyard on his horse, he saw the dead sitting on top of their graves.[138] He also reports that one of his own friends left his house in the city of Āmid in the late afternoon for a garden, and just before sunset he was in the graveyard and saw that one of the graves was on fire, looking like a glass container, with the dead person in the middle. He rubbed his eyes, wondering whether he was awake or asleep. Confused, he turned to the city walls and when he saw them he realised that he could not possibly be asleep. He went home to his family in a daze. They served him food, but he was unable to eat. He went to town inquiring about who the dead man in the grave was and was told he was a tax collector who had died earlier that day.[139]

Shaykh Makīn al-Dīn al-Asmar said, "I spent the night before Fri-

---

i Ibn Qayyim al-Jawziyya, known as Ibn al-Qayyim, was the son of the rector (*qayyim*) of the Jawziyya school of *ḥadīth* in Damascus. Ibn al-Qayyim was a student of Ibn Taymiyya and a prolific author. He died in Damascus in 751 AH.

ii Muṭarrif ibn ʿAbdallāh ibn al-Shakhkhīr al-ʿĀmerī of Baṣra was a scholarly Follower who transmitted *ḥadīth* from ʿAlī and ʿAmmār ibn Yāsir, among others. He died in 95 AH.

day at the Qarāfa.[i] When the visitors started reciting [the Qur'an], I recited along with them, until they got to His saying – August and Majestic is He! – in *Sūra Yūsuf*, ***then Joseph's brothers came***, by which point in their visit they had reached the tomb of Joseph's brothers. As I watched, the grave split open and a man came out. He had a sparse beard, a small head and dark skin. "Who informed you of our tale?" he asked, "for this is how it was."[140]

Ḥabīb ʿAlī ibn ʿAbd al-Raḥmān al-Mashhūr[ii] once went to Say'ūn to attend a gathering of Ḥabīb ʿAlī al-Ḥabashī[iii] for the celebration of the Prophet's birth. He sat to the right of his host and during the proceedings he saw the Prophet ﷺ enter and sit down opposite Ḥabīb ʿAlī al-Ḥabashī. After they were finished, Ḥabīb ʿAlī al-Ḥabashī turned to his guest and whispered in his ear, "Did you see the Prophet?" "Yes," he replied. "How lucky you are!" he said. "Yes, but he sat facing you, not us," he replied. "You have received your share," said Ḥabīb ʿAlī al-Ḥabashī.[141]

In the Christian Gospel, Jesus is said to have gone up the mountain to meet Moses and Elijah. His garments glistened and became intensely white and he was seen conversing with the two other Prophets. The event was witnessed and reported by two of the Apostles, Peter and James.[142]

An Egyptian engineer I have known for a long time in Madina told me a time when he was in serious difficulty, and he went to visit the Prophet's beloved uncle Ḥamza, who was martyred at Uḥud, accompanied by his own uncle. He parked his car and rushed to the graveyard of the martyrs. Before he reached the wall surrounding the graveyard

---

i The Qarāfa Cemetery is the great cemetery of Cairo, at the foot of the Muqaṭṭam Hill, where generations of great scholars and saints are buried. It contains a grave that has been traditionally attributed to one of the brothers of Prophet Joseph.

ii *Ḥabīb* ʿAlī ibn ʿAbd al-Raḥmān al-Mashhūr, who died in 1320 AH, was the son of the great saint, scholar, and *muftī* of Ḥaḍramawt, *Ḥabīb* ʿAbd al-Raḥmān al-Mashhūr (d. 1344 AH) both are well known to have reached the highest degree of sanctity.

iii *Ḥabīb* ʿAlī ibn Muḥammad al-Ḥabashī was a scholar, an eloquent preacher, a talented spiritual poet, and a major saint of Say'ūn, Ḥaḍramawt. He became famous for the large gathering he held each year to celebrate the birth of the Prophet and for the *Mawlid* he authored, *Samṭ al-Durar*, which was chanted during the celebrations.

he was met by a big man who received him with open arms and held him to his chest. He felt the man's heartbeat and smelled a fragrance from his clothes, then he heard him speak to him in a booming voice. In a flash he recognised the man as Ḥamza himself. Moments later the man had let him go and was nowhere to be seen, and his uncle was all over him, smelling his chest, kissing him, greatly excited. He asked him, "What are you doing?" He replied, "Do you think I have not seen him who was holding you?" This is one story of a great many I have heard in Madina about Ḥamza, the Master of all Martyrs.

Imām Aḥmad ibn Ḥanbal's school of jurisprudence was in danger of extinction and was revived by Shaykh ʿAbd al-Qādir al-Jīlānī[i] at the Prophet's bidding.[ii] One day he visited the Imām's grave accompanied by some men of God. They all saw the Imām come out of his grave with a tunic in his hand. He gave the tunic to the Shaykh, they embraced, and then the Imām said, "O *Sayyid* ʿAbd al-Qādir, the science of the *Sharīʿa*, the science of the *Ṭarīqa*, the science of the *Ḥalāl*, and the practice of the *Ḥalāl* are all very much in need of you."[143] This is a clear example of a departed person's spirit appearing in material form in this world and interacting with people. Another example is that of Imām Jalāl al-Dīn al-Suyūṭī's father who, as he was crossing some land being irrigated by the Nile's floodwaters, saw *Sayyid* Aḥmad al-Badawī[iii] approaching on horseback, his face covered with two veils.[144]

Sayyid Aḥmad ibn ʿAbd al-Raḥmān al-Saqqāf of Ḥaḍramawt[iv], who

---

i Shaykh ʿAbd al-Qādir al-Jīlānī, founder of the largest and best known Sufi order, the Qādiriyya, lived in Baghdad, where he died in 561 AH, more than three hundred years after Imām Aḥmad who died in 241 AH. His father is a descendent of Imām Ḥasan, while his mother is a descendent of Imām Ḥusayn. Besides vivifying the Ḥanbalī School, he was also an authority on the Shāfiʿī school of Jurisprudence.

ii ʿShaykh ʿAbd al-Qādir also followed the Shāfiʿī School.

iii *Sayyid* Aḥmad al-Badawī was one of the greatest saints of the 7th century AH. He came from a Ḥusaynī lineage, was born in Morocco, spent his youth in Makka, where he studied the religious sciences, becoming an important transmitter of the various readings of the Qur'ān, before moving to the village of Ṭanṭā at the centre of the Nile Delta in Egypt, where he died and was buried in 675 AH.

iv *Sayyid* Aḥmad ibn ʿAbd al-Raḥmān al-Saqqāf was the son of the chief saint of his day, Imām ʿAbd al-Raḥmān al-Saqqāf Bā-ʿAlawī of Tarīm. Also a great saint, he kept his spiritual rank hidden until he died in 829 A.H.

died in 946 AH, was once told that someone was casting doubts on the authenticity of his ancestor Imām Aḥmad ibn ʿĪsā'si tomb. When he visited the tomb not long afterwards, it was noticed that he went into a state of altered consciousness for a short while, after which he came to and declared, "I have met the spirit of Imām Aḥmad ibn ʿĪsā and asked him if this really was his tomb and he said yes." It was also reported that he met with the spirit of Imām Ghazālī at his home in Tarīm and asked him for an *ijāza* or scholarly authorization in all his works. This having been duly granted and other scholars having heard of it, they requested and received it from *Sayyid* Aḥmad.[145]

A colleague of mine has told me that when his grandmother had died and was attended by his father and her other sons, they dutifully closed her eyes and turned her on to her right side. He then rushed to inform his sisters, choosing to cut across the fields even though it was dark. Suddenly, as he was walking, his grandmother appeared before him and addressed him sharply, "What have you done?" "We have done the right thing," he said, "as we have closed your eyes and turned you on to your right side." "You have turned me on to my left side," she retorted. In a state, he ran back as fast as he could, and breathlessly said to his father, "Let us go in again!" They went in and found that they had indeed inadvertently turned her on to her left side. They immediately rectified her position, but hours later his heart was still racing from the unexpected fright he had experienced.[146]

Just as angels may appear in the material dimension in the form of birds, the spirits of dead saints appear so too. When Ḥabīb ʿAbd al-Raḥmān al-Mashhūr, the famous scholar, saint and Muftī of Ḥaḍramawt, was on his deathbed, he said to his son ʿAlī the day before he died, which was a Friday, "I was to die today, for the *baraka* of Friday, but the folk said they will not come until after sunset." His son asked, "Who are they?" He then whispered in his ear, "The people of the *Barzakh*. However, they say that Prophet Muḥammad ﷺ was taken on his ascent on the night before Saturday. To God does the matter

---

[i] Imām Aḥmad ibn ʿĪsā al-Muhājir is a great grandson of Imām Jaʿfar al-Sādiq who emigrated from Baṣra in Iraq to Ḥaḍramawt. His descendents became the famous Bā-ʿAlawī *sayyids*. He died in 345 A.H.

belong, before and after." He then gave his son instructions on how to prepare and bury him according to the Sacred Law, leaving out no *Sunna* and no recommended practice. He then asked them to forgive him and to ask forgiveness for him, after which he stopped talking to them and kept whispering *Lā ilāha illa'llāh.* They sat next to him until it was time for the maghrib prayer; they then stood up to pray, and once they had started the prayer, three large green birds entered the room and alighted around him. Having finished the prayer they approached to hear what the birds were saying to him and heard the one nearest to his head saying, "Hear him teaching us the *dhikr.*" Then the birds fled. His son and the others could only hear what he was saying by placing their ears right next to his mouth and they heard him repeating *Lā ilāha illa'llāh* until he expired.[147]

3
Manifestations of the Unseen

LIGHTS SHINING FROM THE UNSEEN

Ibn Hishām, the Prophet's biographer, says that as the Prophet's father ʿAbdallāh was walking by the Kaʿba with his father, ʿAbd al-Muṭṭalib, a certain woman – Waraqa ibn Nawfal's sister according to some – looked at his face, then asked him, "Where are you going, ʿAbdallāh?" "Accompanying my father," he replied. She said, "Sleep with me now and I shall give you as many camels as those which have just been slaughtered for you." He answered, "I am with my father now and I cannot leave him." Later on, after he had married Āmina, he passed by the same woman and, surprised that this time she said nothing, asked her why she was not making him the same offer. She answered that the light she had noticed on him that day had left him.[148]

The following stories involving some of the Prophet's Companions should serve to illustrate the pattern with sufficient clarity. Al-Ṭufayl ibn ʿAmr al-Dawsī came to the Prophet ﷺ, complained that his tribe of Daws was resisting his calling them to Islām, and asked him to curse them. Instead, he prayed, "*O God, guide Daws to the truth and bring them to us.*" Then al-Ṭufayl asked for a sign to show his people and the Prophet ﷺ gave him one, for when he reached the pass that would lead him to the dwellings of his tribe, a light shone forth from his forehead. He exclaimed, "O God, do not make it in my face, for they might think it is a curse that befell me for leaving their religion!" The light immediately shifted from his forehead to the tip of his whip, looking like a lantern hanging down from it. This time they all responded to his call and the whole tribe accepted Islām.[149]

Usayd ibn Ḥuḍayr and ʿAbbād ibn Bishr once stayed late with the Prophet ﷺ at his house in Madina. When it was time to go home in the evening, they left the house only to find it was pitch black outside. A light like a lantern then appeared before them, illuminating the road so they were able to walk. When they had to separate, it divided into two, one half going with each of them.[150]

ʿAbdallāh Abū ʿAbs al-Anṣārī used to offer the five ritual prayers with the Prophet ﷺ, then walk to the Banī Ḥāritha area, by which time it was usually late. One dark night his walking stick lit up and he was able to walk by its light until he arrived home safely.[151]

Such events seem to have been common occurrences in the Prophet's time. Some were remembered and transmitted by the Companions to the Followers, who in turn transmitted them to their students and so on, until they found their way into the compilations of *ḥadīth* and were thus preserved, but obviously in many other instances they were not.

Furthermore, there were many such occurrences reported in the days of the Followers. It is reported (for instance) that Thābit al-Bunānī and another man went to visit Muṭarrif ibn ʿAbdallāh ibn al-Shikhkhīr when he was ill and found him unconscious. They were taken aback when three lights suddenly shot out of him: the first from his head, the second from his waist, and the third from his feet. When he regained consciousness they asked him about them and he answered that it had been *Sūra al-Sajda*, that its beginning shone from his head, its middle from his waist, and its conclusion from his feet; and that it was at that very moment ascending to intercede for him. He added that *Sūra Tabārak*[i] was also there guarding him. He then died.[152]

VOICES FROM THE UNSEEN

Another kind of manifestation is that of voices seemingly coming from nowhere. Reliable reports such as the following have been given by the Prophet's Companions, Followers of the Companions and trustworthy scholars throughout the centuries.

Many chronicles record how, when the Prophet ﷺ died, the Companions heard voices saying, "May peace be upon you, O people of the

---

i *Sūra Tabārak* is an alternative name given to *Sūra al-Mulk*, chapter 67 of the Qur'ān. The Prophet ﷺ said about it that it was, *"A sūra of the Qur'ān, thirty verses, which intercedes on behalf of its man until he is forgiven: Tabāraka'lladhī biyadihi'l-mulk."* [Abū Dāwūd, Sunan, 1400; Tirmidhī, Sunan, 2891.]

house, there is in God consolation from every calamity and compensation from every loss. In God place your trust and in God place your hopes, for the deprived is he who has been deprived of reward. And may peace be upon you and the mercy of God and His benedictions."[153]

When they were about to wash the Prophet ﷺ, they were unsure how to proceed. Should they wash him without his clothes as they did with everyone else, or should they leave his clothes on? As they were talking their heads grew heavy and a light sleep overcame them so that their chins rested on their chests. Then someone spoke to them from a corner of the house, whom none of them knew, saying, "Wash the Prophet ﷺ with his clothes on."[154]

The Prophet's Companion ʿImrān ibn Ḥuṣayn confided to one of his students that he was used to seeing the angels coming to greet him, then he asked him not to tell anyone until after he died.[155] The Follower Thābit al-Bunānī said that Ghazāla, ʿImrān's servant, used to say that ʿImrān would bid her to sweep the floor of the house; and as they did so, they used to hear, "*al-salām ʿalaykum*," but saw no one.[156] ʿImrān himself told Thābit that the angels used to greet him with *salām*, until when he became severely ill and permitted his family to treat him with cautery, the greetings stopped. Later on, once he had stopped being cauterised, they resumed. This was because although cautery was recognised by the Arabs as a valid treatment for certain illnesses, it had been declared distasteful by the Prophet who did not like his community to be treated by fire. [157]

Ḥudhayfa ibn al-Yamān said, "As I was praying, I heard someone say, 'O God, Yours is all praise and Yours is all sovereignty. In Your Hand is all good, and to You do all matters return, be they open or secret. You are worthy of perpetual praise, and You have power over all things. O God, forgive me for all my past sins, and protect me in my remaining days, and grant me fragrant works that would please You.' I went to the Prophet ﷺ and said that while I had been praying I had heard someone say all that I had heard. The Messenger of God ﷺ said, '*That was an angel who came to teach you how to praise your Lord – August and Majestic.*'"[158]

Yet another Companion, Abū Mūsā, said that whilst at sea on an expedition, sailing with a good wind and full sails, they heard a voice crying seven times, "O people of the ship, stop so that I may tell you!" Abū Mūsā walked to the prow of the ship and said, "Who are you? Where are you? Can you not see where we are? Can we possibly stop?" The voice answered, "Shall I inform you of what God has decreed upon Himself?" He answered, "Yes." The voice said, "God has decreed upon Himself that whosoever imposes thirst upon himself for the sake of God on a hot day, it shall be incumbent upon God to quench his thirst on the Day of Resurrection." From that time, Abū Mūsā was known to watch for scorching hot days so that he could fast on them.[159]

Ibn Masʿūd said that one day when a man was watering his field he saw a cloud from which he heard a voice saying, "Water the land of so and so." He followed the cloud until he reached the land he had heard named, found its owner there and asked him how he managed it. The man answered that he was used to dividing his revenue in three: a third to be used for the needs of the land, a third to be given away in charity, and a third to be kept for his family.[160]

A man of the third generation, that of the Followers of the Followers, Wuhayb ibn al-Ward who died in 153 AH said, "I was circumambulating the House one night with Sufyān al-Thawrī after *ʿishā'*, and when we finished we entered the *Ḥijr* and prayed. Thereafter Sufyān started another circumambulation while I stayed behind to pray. Then I heard a voice from the direction of the House and its covering cloth, saying, "To God – August and Exalted is He! – do I complain, O Gabriel," then it went on to complain about the suffering the Kaʿba endures in hearing the trivial conversation of the people ambling around it.[161]

The traditionist Ibn Abi'l-Dunyā[i] authored a treatise devoted to these "voices from the Unseen" or *hawātif*, as they are known in Arabic, in which he narrates many stories where words are heard by the physical ear, but no one is seemingly around who could have spoken them. One of these stories occurred during the caliphate of ʿUmar ibn al-Khaṭṭāb, when a severe drought afflicted the people and he led them out to the

---

i ʿAbdallāh ibn Muḥammad ibn Abi'l-Dunyā of Baghdad who died in 281 AH was a *Ḥāfiẓ* of *ḥadīth* who authored over 160 books, mostly compilations of *ḥadīth*, each volume dealing with a single subject.

muṣallā to pray for rain.[i] Before he prayed he folded his upper garment over as he had seen the Prophet ﷺ do. Sure enough, before he had left the *muṣallā*, it began to rain. Later on, a Bedouin came to Madina, saying, "O Commander of the Faithful, we were in our valley on such and such a day, when a cloud came over us and we heard a voice in it saying, 'Succour has come, O Abū Ḥafṣ, succour has come!"

Thābit al-Bunānī said that when he was standing on ʿArafāt he saw two young men, one of whom said to the other, "Do you think that He for Whose sake we have loved and befriended each other shall torment us tomorrow in our graves?" They heard the voice of someone they could not see saying, "No, He will not!" He also recounted that as he was walking in the cemetery a voice from behind him said, "O Thābit, do not deceived by the silence for how many an aggrieved soul is abiding here!" He turned around and no one was there.

ʿUmar ibn ʿAbd al-ʿAzīz, the fifth Rightly-Guided Caliph, was not only one of the major scholars of his time, but also a saintly man of God. Once, at the cemetery, he heard the dust speaking to him, describing to him what had happened to the loved ones buried there over the years, and how their bodies had been decomposed. ʿUmar wept profusely as he listened, until finally he was asked, "Shall I tell you of shrouds that never rot?" "What are they?" he asked, and was told, "The fear of God and good works."[162]

Mālik ibn Dīnār[ii] recounted that he once went to visit one of his neighbours who had fallen ill. He counselled him saying, "Promise God – August and Majestic is He! – that you shall repent so that He may cure you." He replied, "Such a hope is so remote! O Abū Yaḥyā, I am dead, for in fact I wished to promise as I used to before, but this time I heard a voice coming from the side of the House, saying, 'We have accepted your pledges before, but found you to be a liar.'" No sooner had Mālik left the house than he heard them weeping over him.

Imām Aḥmad ibn Ḥanbal was arrested in Baghdad and jailed for

---

i The *muṣallā* is the open ground west of the great mosque in Madina, where the Prophet used to hold his ʿĪd prayers on a regular basis, as well as certain other prayers on occasion, such as prayers for rain and some funeral prayers.

ii Mālik ibn Dīnār was a Follower and transmitter of *ḥadīth*. He was mostly famous for his asceticism and sanctity. He lived in Baṣra and died in 131 AH.

refusing to concede that the Qur'ān was created and persisting in saying that it was the uncreated Word of God.[i] The Muʿtazilites had convinced the Abbasid caliph to adopt their creed and impose it by force. The theological argument between them and the majority *Ahl al-Sunna* was raging. As the traditionist Saʿīd ibn Manṣūr[ii] was circumambulating the Kaʿba, he heard a voice saying, "Today Aḥmad ibn Ḥanbal was flogged." He asked his companion, "Did you hear that?" He answered, "Yes." He said, "This is either an angel or one of the virtuous jinn. If this is true, Aḥmad ibn Ḥanbal was beaten today." Eventually, news came to confirm what they had heard.[163]

Ibrāhīm al-Khawwāṣ[iii] recounted how he had once been travelling on a desert road on his way to Makka. He was told there was a mighty lion nearby and this scared him. Then he heard a voice saying, "Steady! There are seventy thousand angels around you that are protecting you."[164]

Shaykh Ḥusayn al-Dajānī[iv], who died in 1274 AH, was a scholar and Sufi, and held the office of Muftī of Jaffa in Palestine. His son Shaykh Muḥammad said that his mother had told him that on at least two occasions his father had heard a voice commanding him to get up and go out to receive his guests. On one occasion, in 1273 AH he told his wife after *fajr* prayer that he had heard someone saying to him, "Get up, Ḥusayn, and go meet one of God's saints." He asked her to prepare food and lodgings, then set out to meet the guest, still not knowing whom it might be. As he walked he saw one of his students hurrying

---

i Imām Aḥmad ibn Ḥanbal was a foremost scholar and traditionist, founder of one of the four schools of Sunnī jurisprudence that exist today. He lived in Baghdad and died in 241 AH.

ii Saʿīd ibn Manṣūr was a traditionist who was born in Balkh and lived in Makka, learning *ḥadīth* from such illustrious scholars as Imām Mālik and Imām al-Layth ibn Saʿd, and who taught important traditionists such as Muslim, Abū Dāwūd and Aḥmad ibn Ḥanbal. He died in Makka in 227 AH.

iii Ibrāhīm al-Khawwāṣ was a famous Sufi mentioned by Qushayrī in his Risāla, who died 291 AH.

iv Shaykh Ḥusayn ibn Salīm al-Dajānī is a Palestinian scholar who was born in Jaffa in 1202 AH. He is a Ḥusaynī *sharīf* who comes from a long line of saintly scholars and who studied in Palestine, then in the Azhar University. He practiced Shāfi'ī *Fiqh*, but was also an authority on Ḥanafī *Fiqh*. He died in Makka in 1274 AH.

toward him, saying that *Sayyid* ʿAbd al-Qādir al-Jazāʾirī[i] had just entered town. The second occasion occurred when the arrival of Shaykh Maḥmūd al-Rāfiʿī al-Ṭarābulsī[ii] was announced to him.[165]

OTHER SOUNDS FROM THE UNSEEN

Events involving higher realities in the unseen dimensions produce various sounds that when described by those capable of perceiving them are necessarily described in terms of earthly sounds. For example, the Prophet ﷺ said that when God speaks the Revelation, the denizens of heaven hear a clatter resembling that of a chain being dragged over a rock. They remain thus until Gabriel arrives and when he does their hearts regain awareness and they ask, "O Gabriel, what has your Lord said?" He replies, "The truth," and they repeat after him, "The truth, the truth."[166] And when asked about how Revelation comes to him, the Prophet ﷺ answered that sometimes it comes like the ringing of a bell, which is when it comes inwardly to his heart, which is the most exhausting to him, and sometimes the angel takes on a human form and speaks to him.[167]

Ḥakīm ibn Ḥizām, who was on the pagan side on the Day of Badr, later recounted that when the Prophet ﷺ threw the dirt in their faces they heard a sound like that of pebbles falling from the sky into a metal basin, which heralded their defeat.[168] Again, on the Day of Ḥunayn, the Prophet ﷺ took a handful of dirt and threw it in the face of the enemy saying, "*Befouled be the faces!*" Those who were in the enemy ranks later recounted how their eyes and mouths were filled with dirt and how they heard a clattering sound in the air, similar to that made by an iron chain being rattled over an iron basin.[169] That on both occasions the dirt reached the eyes and mouths of practically all the enemy warriors was obviously the miraculous part of the event. The accompany-

---

i Better known as Emir ʿAbd al-Qādir, this Ḥasanī *sharīf* led the fight against the French occupation forces for seventeen years in Algeria in the 19th century. He was a scholar and Sufi and when defeated spent the last years of his life in Damascus authoring Sufi books until his death in 1300 AH.

ii No biographical data were found for Shaykh Maḥmūd al-Rāfiʿī al-Ṭarābulsī except in the context of the biography of Shaykh Ḥusayn al-Dajānī where he is said to be a scholar and saint who frequented the Shaykh.

ing sounds, described as pebbles falling into a metal basin in the first instance and as iron being rattled over iron in the second, are obviously manifestations from the World of Similitudes (*ʿĀlam al-Mithāl*).

Abū Hurayra said that once when they were with the Prophet ﷺ they heard a loud bump. The Prophet ﷺ asked them, "*Do you know what that was?*" They answered, "God and His Messenger know best." He said, "*That was a stone that had been thrown into the Fire seventy autumns ago. It was still plummeting into the Fire and had just reached the bottom.*"[170] The sound that all the Companions heard was coming from Hell. Nevertheless, both the Prophet ﷺ and the Companions heard it as they hear the physical sounds of this world, the difference being that while the Companions heard it but did not know what it was, the Prophet ﷺ, through his superior powers of unveiling, knew exactly what had happened.

IMAGES FROM THE UNSEEN

Once during the days of the persecution in Makka, the Prophet's archenemy Abū Jahl decided to bring a large rock and throw it at the Prophet's back as he prostrated before the Kaʿba. But suddenly he was stopped in his tracks and retreated in haste. His face had turned very pale and the rock fell from his hands. The men of Quraysh rose and exclaimed, "What is with you, O Abu'l-Ḥakam?" He said, "I was going towards him to do what I vowed yesterday I would do, but when I approached him I saw a trench of fire, terror and wings!" The Prophet ﷺ said, "*Had he come any nearer the angels would have torn him apart.*"[171]

ʿAlī was asked, "O Commander of the Faithful, tell me about this House. Is it the first house to be erected for the people?" He replied, "There were houses before it – Noah lived in houses – but it was the first house made for the people to be a blessing and a guidance." He was asked, "Tell me about how it was built." He said, "God revealed to Abraham, 'Build a house for Me,' and Abraham was at a loss for what to do, so God sent a wind named *Sakīna* and also *Khajūj*, which had two eyes and a head; and God revealed to Abraham that he was to follow it wherever it went, halting whenever it halted. It moved until it reached the location of the House and curled itself up like a shield, opposite the Populous House *(al-Bayt al-Maʿmūr)*, which is entered by seventy thousand angels every day, none of whom will ever return to it till Resurrection Day."[172]

Ibn ʿAbbās said that when Adam was sent down from Paradise to earth, he missed the voices of heaven and felt estranged, so he complained to his Lord, saying, "O Lord, why do I no longer hear the angels?" He was told, "Because of your sin, Adam. But go and build Me a house, circumambulate it and remember Me, as you have seen the angels doing around my Throne." Having thus been directed toward Makka, Adam began walking. The earth was folded up for him, with each step he crossed a wilderness and wherever he placed his foot the place was blessed and a township arose. When he reached Makka, God sent down a tent from heaven, a hollow red ruby the corners of which were white, the size of which was about the house of the Kaʿba that we know, but the height of which reached up to heaven, to be placed at the location of the House. There were three lanterns of gold inside it and it was lit up with the light of Paradise. With it the corner was sent down, which was a white ruby from Paradise. The angels stood guard around the sanctuary to prevent the then denizens of the earth, at that time the jinn, from penetrating. They stood where the boundaries of the *Ḥaram* or Sanctuary were later demarcated by Abraham.[173]

One day a jurist, who had committed the Qur'ān to memory, skipped a passage while reciting in Shaykh Muḥammad al-Farghal's[i] presence. He immediately stopped him, exclaiming, "You have jumped!" "How did you know I jumped when you have not memorised the Qur'ān?" He answered, "I was witnessing a light ascending to heaven, when suddenly it was disrupted and was no longer seen to be ascending. At this I knew that you had jumped."[174]

Sayyid Muḥammad Rāshid Metwallī, who died in 2013 CE, a judge and former Vice-Minister of Justice in Egypt, told me that in his younger days his teacher Shaykh Aḥmad Riḍwān told him that he had seen a light extending from him to Imām Ḥasan. Then a while later

i Shaykh Muḥammad ibn Aḥmad al-Farghal is an Egyptian saint who was well known for his sanctity among the Sufi community, but was not a scholar. He died in the 850's AH.

he told him he had seen a light extending from him to Imām Ḥusayn. The significance of this was that he was a descendent of both Imāms, which until that point in time was unknown to him. That had happened at the Shaykh's headquarters near Luxor in Upper Egypt. As soon as he returned to Cairo, *Sayyid* Muḥammad asked his mother about it and she told him that his parents were indeed descended from the two Imāms, one of them from Imām Ḥasan and the other from Imām Ḥusayn.

The Prophet ﷺ said, "*God created Adam, rubbed his back with His right Hand, extracting progeny from it, and then said, 'These I have created for the Garden and the works of the people of the Garden they shall do.' Again He rubbed his back, extracting more progeny, and then He said, 'These I have created for the Fire and the works of the people of the Fire they shall do.'*"[175]

FRAGRANCES FROM THE UNSEEN

ʿAbdallāh ibn Ghālib was a Follower who transmitted *ḥadīth* from the Companion Abū Saʿīd al-Khudrī. He was an ascetic who lived in Baṣra and died in battle in 83 AH. No sooner had they laid him in his grave than they smelled the strong scent of musk. His student Mālik ibn Dīnār – the famous ascetic, scholar and saint – said that when he took a handful of dust from his grave, he found it to be musk. The people became so fascinated by this phenomenon that the authorities had to level his grave to make it unrecognisable.[176]

The fragrance of musk was also smelled from the grave of the great traditionist Imām Bukhārī. The man who gave him hospitality during the last days of his life recounts that once they had prayed the funeral prayer, and placed him in his grave, a fragrance like that of musk rose from the dust. It lasted for days and people kept taking the dust of the grave until a wooden lattice was eventually erected around it.[177]

Similar stories abound in the literature, making the appearance of perfumed fragrances around the graves of saints a fairly common occurrence. Over the years, I have personally known and still know a number of persons who smell a perfumed scent whenever they visit the graves of *Sayyidunā* Ḥamza and the martyrs of Uḥud. Sometimes the experience is shared by those in their company and sometimes not.

MATERIALISATIONS FROM THE UNSEEN

According to Jābir, a solar eclipse once occurred in Madina on a very hot day. The Prophet ﷺ led his Companions in a special prayer, the eclipse prayer, and stood up for so long that they nearly collapsed. Then they saw him take a sudden step backward, then a while later extend his hand forward as if to grasp something. When the prayer was over he explained what had happened, saying, "*I beheld the Fire, and this is when you saw me step back for fear of being touched by its heat. Then I saw the Garden, and this is when you saw me reach out, for I thought to pluck a bunch of grapes, but then thought better of it.*"[178] Again the episode shows how far from being mere illusions these visions are, as does the following example. The Companion Khubayb was captured by the Makkan pagans and imprisoned in Makka before he was taken out of the sacred territory and killed. His captors found him eating grapes when there was none at all in Makka at the time.[179]

A man reported to the Prophet ﷺ that two women had been fasting until they were nearly dead of thirst. He gave him no answer. The man returned at high noon saying, "O Prophet of God, they are dead or nearly so." So he said, "*Call them.*" When they came he asked for a cup and told one of them, "*Throw up!*" She brought up blood and pus, filling half the cup. Then he told the other, "*Throw up!*" She brought up similar stuff and raw meat, until she had filled the rest of the cup. He said, "*These two are fasting from what God has permitted but have eaten what He has forbidden. They sat together eating the flesh of others.*"[180] Here is an intelligible reality, which is the reality of backbiting and slander and what they mean in terms of real values rather than some words uttered in the physical dimension. They take on an appropriately horrendous material form, which was clearly perceived by all who were present at this scene.

The Qur'ān describes an episode when the Apostles requested their master Jesus to ask his Lord to provide them with food from Heaven: ***And when the apostles said, "O Jesus, son of Mary, is your Lord able to send down on us a table from Heaven?"*** They said they wished to eat from it so that the miracle would strengthen their certitude and they would celebrate the event as a feast for them and coming generations. Jesus responded to their plea: ***He prayed, "O God, our Lord, send down upon us a table from Heaven."***[181] The commentaries specify that the food that was made to descend from Heaven to them was made of fish and bread. The 'Descent from Heaven' is to be understood as the materialisation of higher realities from the Unseen into physical forms.

Another such event reported by the Qur'ān concerns Mary, whose guardian was the Prophet Zachariah: ***Whenever Zachariah went in to her in her seclusion he found her provisioned.***[182] Commentators say he found winter fruits in the summer and summer fruits in the winter. He asked her where this came from and she answered that: ***God gives whomsoever He chooses without reckoning.***[183]

Anas reports two occasions when water gushed between the Prophet's fingers in such a quantity that all the Companions who had been there were able to perform their ritual ablutions with it. He said, "The Prophet ﷺ was brought a vessel, as he was standing in the Zawrā' area. He dipped his hand in the vessel and water started gushing from between his fingers, until all the people had performed their ablutions." When asked how many were there, Anas answered that there were about three hundred.[184] On another occasion (in the mosque) the time for prayer came, and those whose houses were near the mosque rose to do their ablutions, while about eighty men remained. The Prophet ﷺ brought a stone pot containing a small amount of water, and tried to put his hand into it, but found its mouth to be too narrow. However, he managed to get his hand in by joining his fingers together. He dipped them into the water and everyone did their ablutions.[185] There are eight such instances alone in the compilation of Bukhārī and many more in the other books of *ḥadīth*.

Food is also reported to have once increased on Abū Bakr's table when he had guests.[186]

Umm Ayman, a slave who looked after the Prophet ﷺ as a child, whom he inherited when his father died and then freed when he married Khadīja, emigrated from Makka to join the Prophet ﷺ in Madina. She came on foot, carrying no provisions, and was fasting. It was a very hot day and as she reached Rawḥā' she became very dehydrated and extremely thirsty. Shortly after sunset, as she was on the verge of dying from thirst, she heard a rustling sound above her head. Looking up, there was a bucket of water hanging from a rope drawing nearer to her. She grasped it and drank from it until she was satiated. Since that day she found that she could fast in hot weather and walk about in the sun, yet never feel thirst.[187]

Ibn ʿAbbās recounts how a woman named Umm Sharīk, having accepted Islām in Makka, began to visit the Makkan women and talk to them convincingly about Islām. Eventually news of the matter spread in Makka. The Makkans arrested Umm Sharīk and threatened to torture her, before deciding to exile her to Madina. They placed her on a camel, set off for Madina, and for three days left her with neither food nor drink. Whenever they stopped to rest, they tied her up and left her in the sun, while they sat in the shade. One day, as she was left in the sun, she felt something very cold on her chest. She found it to be a bucket of water and drank from it a little, but then it was raised up beyond her reach. Then many times over it came down again and she drank a little more. Finally, it came down and remained with her so that she was able to drink her fill and pour the rest on her body and clothes. When the party awakened they found her looking fresh, with traces of moisture still on her clothes. They said, "You cut yourself loose, took our water skins and drank the water in them." She swore she had not and told them what had happened. They exclaimed that if she told the truth, then her religion must be better than theirs. On inspection, they found their water skins to be full. At this, they accepted Islām and conveyed her safely to Madina.[188]

A woman who was visiting ʿĀ'isha, the Prophet's wife, said, "I have given my oath to the Messenger of God ﷺ not to associate anything with God, not to steal, not to commit adultery, not to kill my children, not to commit anything evil with my hands and feet, and not to disobey when enjoined to do some good. I have kept my pledge to my Lord and my Lord will keep His pledge to me, so that, by God, He shall not punish me!" Later on in her sleep an angel came to her saying, "Not so! You embellish yourself to excess and reveal your beauty; you deny the good that is done to you; you offend your neighbour and you disobey your husband." Then he placed his five fingers on her face, saying, "Five for five. If you say more, we shall do more." In the morning, the traces of the fingers were to be seen on her face.[189]

The Prophet ﷺ said, "*When the Muslim rinses his mouth as he performs his ritual ablution, his sins come out of his mouth; when he snuffs water, they come out of his nostrils; when he washes his face, they come out of his face; when he washes his hands, they come out of his hands, even going from under his fingernails; when he rubs his scalp, they come out of his scalp, even coming out of his ears; when he washes his feet, they come out from his feet, even from under his toenails; and when he heads toward the prayer, his walking to the mosque is equivalent to praying, while his prayer is supererogation.*"[190] This *ḥadīth* indicates that sins have subtle forms that exit from the body during ablutions. We have heard from many a man of God that these can be seen by them.

Ibn ʿAbbās died in Ṭā'if and his funeral was attended by many eminent Followers, such as Saʿīd ibn Jubayr and Mujāhid. They all reported – as recounted earlier – seeing a strange white bird fly along and enter into Ibn ʿAbbās's shroud. They waited for it to come out, but it did not. Once he had been buried, they heard a voice recite: ***O tranquil soul, return to your Lord.***[191]

Yaʿqūb ibn ʿAbdallāh ibn al-Ashajj[i] was one of the good men of this community. He saw in his dream that he was admitted to Paradise and given milk to drink. He was on a naval expedition at sea, where obviously no milk was available. One of his companions said to him, "I beseech you by God to bring up what is in your belly!" So he vomited bright white milk. That was on the day he was killed.[192]

Imām al-Layth ibn Saʿd[ii] went for pilgrimage in 113 AH and walked all the way to Makka. One day, after praying *ʿaṣr*, he walked up the hill of Abū Qubays and saw a man sitting there, calling upon his Lord and saying,

---

i Yaʿqūb ibn ʿAbdallāh ibn al-Ashajj was a Follower and reliable transmitter of *ḥadīth*. He died at sea in 122 AH.

ii Al-Layth ibn Saʿd was an independent scholar, a *mujtahid imām*, which means that he followed no other scholar in their rulings, but was able to derive them directly from the sources, which are the Qur'ān and the *Sunna* of the Prophet. There were letters between him and Imām Mālik debating certain legal issues. He died in Egypt in 175 AH.

"O Lord! O Lord!" until he ran out of breath. He then cried, "My Lord! My Lord!" until breathless. And then he cried, "O Allāh!" until he ran out of breath, then, "O Living! O Living!", then "O Infinitely Merciful! O Infinitely Merciful!", then "O Compassionate! O Compassionate!", then "O Most Merciful of the merciful! O Most Merciful of the merciful!" until he ran out of breath several times. Then he said, "O God, I desire grapes, so feed me grapes, and my shawls are worn out." Layth then continued, "No sooner had he spoken than I saw a basket full of grapes, when there were no grapes at all in the land at that time, and I also saw two shawls placed beside him. He was about to eat when I said, "I am your partner." "How is that so?" he asked. I said, "Because you were praying and I was saying,' 'Amen!'" He said, "Come closer then and eat, but take none of it away with you." I ate with him. I ate seedless grapes with him; they tasted like nothing I had eaten before. I ate until satiated, yet the basket remained as it was. He said, "Take the shawl you like best." I said, "As for the shawls, I have no need for them." He said, "Step aside so that I can change into them," which I did. He wrapped one around his waist and the other around his shoulders, then he took the two old ones and started down the hill. I followed him until we reached the Masʿa.[i] A man came up to him there saying, "Clothe me, O son of the Messenger of God! May God clothe you in the raiment of Paradise!" He said to me, "Give them to him." I went to the man and gave them to him and then asked him, "Who is this?" He said, "Jaʿfar ibn Muḥammad."[ii] I went back to him hoping to hear something from him that might profit me, but he was nowhere to be found.[193]

---

i The Masʿa is an area between the two hills of Safā and Marwa, not far from the Kaʿba. During the pilgrimage, this is where the rite of *saʿy* must be performed, which is to walk seven times between the two hills.

ii Jaʿfar ibn Muḥammad is Imām Jaʿfar al-Sādiq son of Imām Muḥammad al-Bāqir, son of Imām ʿAlī Zayn al-ʿĀbidīn, son of Imām al-Ḥusayn – may God be pleased with them.

A HIGHER REALITY

4
Images of Remote Realities

IMAGES OF REALITIES REMOTE IN SPACE

When the Prophet ﷺ returned from his Night Journey and related what he had seen to the Quraysh, they refused to believe him, and challenged him to describe the Bayt al-Maqdis in Jerusalem, now known as the Aqṣā Mosque. No sooner had he begun to do so than he realised he would be unable to remember it as accurately as he would have wished; therefore, God brought its image before him so that he was able to describe all of its details. He also explained to them the Prophets he had met there before his Ascension and how he had led them in prayer.[194] In Aḥmad's version there is the further detail that the temple was brought so near that it was just before the house of ʿAqīl, ʿAlī's brother.[195] On this occasion, the Prophet ﷺ explicitly stated that an image of the temple was shown to him, which is clearly a manifestation of the *ʿĀlam al-Mithāl.* Had he simply stated that he had seen it, there would have been the possibility that he meant he had seen its physical form even as it stood in Jerusalem by his powers of unveiling. On the other hand, his vision of the other Prophets and his leading them in prayer in Bayt al-Maqdis undoubtedly belongs to the *ʿĀlam al-Mithāl* and clearly shows how real this world is.[196]

IMAGES FROM THE FUTURE

Time, as we know, is relative. The medium of the *ʿĀlam al-Mithāl* allows certain spirits to witness events from both the past and the future, in the form of dream-visions for most people, but for some as waking visions.

Standing amidst his Companions on a rooftop in Madina, the Prophet ﷺ said, "*Do you see what I see? I see sedition falling on your houses like rainfall.*"[197] We know from this *ḥadīth* that the Prophet ﷺ saw the sedition that was to befall his community after him. It is no wonder, then, that we have countless other *ḥadīth*s describing it in detail. One of these will describe the African man destined to wreak destruction upon the Kaʿba at the end of time. He said of him ﷺ in one *ḥadīth* that he was thin legged and in another, "*It is as if I saw him, black, bow-legged, demolishing it stone by stone.*"[198] We have already mentioned some of the *ḥadīth*s concerning the Dajjāl and the second coming of Jesus. Another *ḥadīth* concerning both the condition of the community at the end of time and the Hereafter states, "*I shall precede and wait for you and I shall be a witness against you. By God, I can now see my Basin. I have been given the keys to the treasuries of the earth; and by God, I have no fear that you will associate with God after me, but I fear that you will compete for it.*"[199] Here the Prophet ﷺ explicitly states that he saw his Basin which is something we know that God will only give him on the Day of Judgement.

IMAGES FROM THE HEREAFTER

The Day of Resurrection shall be a time when the manifestations of the World of Similitudes shall be the rule rather than the exception, for everything will then appear according to its inner reality. For instance, as the Prophet ﷺ said, "*The arrogant will be brought on the Day of Resurrection as minute ants in the form of men, surrounded from all sides with abasement.*"[200] This means that the punishment of the arrogant will appropriately be the opposite of their crime, and they shall be made to suffer diminution in size and humiliation.

The Prophet ﷺ described in great detail many of the happenings that will occur on the Day of Resurrection. These descriptions make it obvious that such occurrences would have been impossible in the world of solid forms, namely our worldly life, and that the conditions of the Day of Resurrection and what follows it are entirely different and correspond to the conditions of a world of subtler and more fluid forms. Among what he ﷺ said is the following, "*Once the people of the Garden have entered the Garden and the people of the Fire [have entered] the Fire, God – exalted is He! – will say, 'Bring out of the Fire those in whose hearts is a mustard seed's weight of faith.' They will come out of it all blackened and shall be cast into the River of Life from whence they shall sprout just as a seed on the side of the floodplain sprouts. Have you not seen it coming out, yellow, winding?*"[201] He ﷺ also said that on Judgement Day some men shall be called and given their records in their right hands. Their bodies will be made sixty cubits tall, their faces will whiten, and crowns of sparkling pearls shall be placed on their heads. As for the disbelievers, they will also be made sixty cubits tall, but their faces will be blackened, and they shall have evil crowns placed on their heads.[202]

Moreover, realities that had been unseen in this life will then be manifest for all to see. On that day, for example, as the Prophet ﷺ said, the two greatest *sūras* in the Qur'ān, *Sūra al-Baqara* and *Sūra Āl ʿImrān*, which he called the "*two radiant ones*", will come in the form of clouds to intercede on behalf of and defend those who had recited them often.[203] And he ﷺ said that fasting and the Qur'ān both intercede for the servant on Judgement Day. The fast will say, "O Lord, I have kept him from food and sexual appetite by day, so allow me to intercede for him!" and the Qur'ān will say, "I have kept him from sleeping at night, so allow me to intercede for him." And their intercession will be allowed.[204] He ﷺ also said that those who had been faithfully prostrating themselves before God in this world will be able to do so on Judgement Day, while those who did so only out of ostentation will find that their backs remain stiff, preventing them from prostrating themselves.[205] According to the laws of the World of Similitudes, what is inwardly hidden in the material dimension becomes outwardly manifest there. The intention of the hypocrites in this world was to prostrate themselves before God ostentatiously to show others that they are devout Muslims, while in their hearts either rejecting Islām altogether or accepting it in a shallow manner. This intention will be manifest on Judgement Day as an inability to bow or prostrate, bringing the rejection in the heart out into the open for all to see.

The Prophet ﷺ asked Ubayy ibn Kaʿb, "*Which verse of the Book of God is greatest?*" He answered many times over, "God and His Messenger know best." Then he said, "The Verse of the Pedestal." The Prophet ﷺ said, "*May your knowledge be your delight, O Abu'l-Mundhir! By He in Whose Hand is my soul, it has a tongue and two lips that glorify God at the foot of the Throne.*"[206]

The Prophet ﷺ also said that, "*Death will be brought in the form of a fair ram and a herald will cry, 'O People of the Garden,' at which they will extend their necks and gaze. He will ask them, 'Do you recognise this one?' They will answer, 'Yes, this is Death.' Then he will call the people of the Fire, ask them the same question and receive the same answer. Then it will be slaughtered, and he will announce, 'O People of the Garden, perpetual life, for death is no longer. O People of the Fire, perpetual life, for death is no longer.'*" Then the Prophet ﷺ recited, "***And warn them of the Day of Remorse when the matter will have been decided while they are unaware and do not believe.***" He then waved with his hand, giving them to understand that the unaware are the people of this world.[207]

The Prophet ﷺ said, "*Camels shall come to their owner, in as good a shape as they had ever been; but if he had failed to fulfil their rights, they will trample him with their hooves. Sheep will also come to their owner, in as good a shape as they had ever been; but if he had failed to fulfil their rights, they will trample him with their hooves and butt him with their horns.*"[208] The rights of camels, sheep and other domestic animals is to pay out the *zakāt* due on them in full and in time, look after them adequately, give of their milk to the poor, and use the camel to carry riders to fight in the way of God.

The Prophet ﷺ also said that there is a market in the Garden where there is neither buying nor selling, but only images of men and women. When a man desires an image, he simply assumes it.[209] This is evidently one of those phenomena that would be inconceivable had the density and opaqueness of the people of the Garden matched their condition in this life.

Among the things that are hidden in this world except for the people of unveiling, but will appear for everyone to see on Resurrection Day, are the lights of believers. The Prophet ﷺ informed his community that he will recognise them on Resurrection Day because they will have light on their foreheads, forearms and hands, and feet, which are the areas they used to wash in their ritual ablutions in the world.[210]

ʿAbdallāh ibn Masʿūd explained the verse, ***Their light running before them***, saying, "They are given their lights according to their works: the light of some of them is as a mountain, while the light of the least among them appears on his thumb, flaring up at times and dimming at others."[211] In another version, ʿAbdallāh ibn Masʿūd said he had heard the Prophet ﷺ say that some will be given a light as large as an immense mountain, others less than that, others like a palm tree in his right hand, others smaller than that, and others will be given a light on their big toes that shines and they are able to walk, then fades away so that they must stop. When they have to cross the Bridge (*Ṣirāṭ*), they will cross with a speed in proportion to their lights: some will cross in the blink of an eye, others like lightning, others like clouds, others like a shooting star, others like the wind, others like a galloping horse, others like a running man, until he who had been given a light on his big toe will cross crawling.[212]

The Prophet ﷺ said that on Judgement Day a group of people filling the entire horizon shall come, whose light will be like that of the sun. Every Prophet will then be eager to find out whether they are his community, but it will be said they are Muḥammad ﷺ and his community. Then another group will come, whose light will be like that of the moon, then another like stars in the sky.[213]

5
Voices Carrying for Vast Distances

Ibn ʿAbbās relates an extraordinary event concerning the first call to the pilgrimage, which was made by Abraham almost four millennia ago. He said that when Abraham had completed building the House, he said, "O God, I am finished." So he was ordered, "Proclaim the pilgrimage!" He said, "Lord, how far will my voice carry?" God said, "Yours is the proclamation and Mine is to make it carry." He asked, "Lord, what shall I say?" He said, "Say, 'O people, the pilgrimage has been prescribed for you, the pilgrimage to the Ancient House.'"[214] Those who answered the call affirmatively on that day, even while still in the World of Spirits and long before their descent in this world, when the time comes for them in this worldly life will be those who perform the pilgrimage. Those who answered once will perform it once; those who answered twice will perform it twice, and so on.

The following event occurred during the caliphate of ʿUmar ibn al-Khaṭṭāb. ʿUmar had sent an army to Persia in 23 AH under the command of a man named Sāriya. One day as he was standing on the pulpit delivering a sermon at the Prophet's Mosque in Madina, he caused great surprise among his audience by crying, "The hill, Sāriya, the hill!" Sometime afterward, Sāriya sent a messenger from Persia to ʿUmar to inform him that they had heard a voice crying, "Sāriya, the hill!" as they were about to be attacked and defeated. They had consequently retreated to the nearby hill to protect their rear and eventually came out victorious.[215] We are faced with two supernatural events here: the first being that ʿUmar was able to see the army in Persia whilst on the pulpit in Madina in a fully awakened state, which pertains to unveiling. The second was that his voice could reach them, which pertains to the World of Similitudes. We take note of the fact that he knew perfectly well that his voice would reach them; otherwise there would have been no point in his calling out. The implication is that for people like ʿUmar these powers are quite natural, although other less fortunate persons may consider them to be supernatural.

6
Witnessing the Jinn

According to the Qur'ān, the jinn served Solomon, and worked under his supervision.[216]

The episode of the jinn in Makka before the Emigration involves the waking state vision of two kinds of normally invisible created beings. First, the Prophet ﷺ meets with a group of jinn, whom his Companion Ibn Masʿūd also sees, but is not allowed to meet. He spends most of the night speaking with them and invites them to Islām. Once this is over, the Prophet ﷺ then returns to Ibn Masʿūd and, feeling tired, rests his head on his thigh and goes to sleep. The Companion then sees men in white standing and conversing near the Prophet ﷺ as he sleeps. These men in white turn out to be angels. When he wakes up, the Prophet ﷺ asks his Companion, "*Have you heard what they have said? Do you know who they are?*" He answers, "God and his Messenger know better." He says, "*They were angels.*"[217] Thus, the same reality witnessed by the fully awake Ibn Masʿūd was also seen by the Prophet ﷺ in his sleep. For Prophets, of course, there is no great difference between their perceptions in the waking state or during sleep. The Prophet ﷺ once said to ʿĀ'isha, "*My eyes sleep, but my heart does not.*"[218]

THE PROPHETS SEEING SATAN

We have learnt from the above that jinn can be seen and spoken to. Those that are evil among the jinn are called devils and the same applies to them. God's Prophet Abraham saw the chief devil, Satan or Iblīs, many times. According to Ibn ʿAbbās, the Prophet ﷺ said, "*When Abraham the Friend was performing his rites, the Devil came to him near Jamrat al-ʿAqaba. He stoned him with seven pebbles, until he sunk into the ground. Then he came to him close to the second Jamra, and he again stoned him with seven pebbles, until he sunk into the ground. Then he came to him in the proximity of the third Jamra, and yet again he stoned him with seven pebbles, until he sunk into the ground.*"[219] Similarly, Ibn ʿAbbās reports that Gabriel came to the Prophet ﷺ, and took him to demonstrate the pilgrimage rites. Three times, as he approached each of the three Jamra, the Devil appeared to him, and three times he stoned him with seven pebbles until he sunk into the ground. Then he went away.[220]

According to Muslim tradition, Jesus is also reported to have seen the Devil. According to Abu'l-Hudhayl, "When the Devil saw Jesus – may peace be upon him – on the mountain in Jerusalem, he said to him, 'You claim you can revive the dead, so pray to God that he may turn this mountain into bread.' Jesus answered, 'Do all people live only by bread?' So he said, 'If you are as you say, jump from here for the angels will catch you.' He said, 'My Lord has commanded me not to try myself, for I know not whether He will save me or not.'"[221] In another version, according to Ṭāwūs, the Devil says, "You know that nothing will happen to you save what has already been decided for you, so climb to the summit of this mountain and throw yourself down to see whether you will live or not." Jesus answered, "Do you not know that God has said, 'Let not my servant try Me, for I do as I please' or – according to Zuhrī – 'The servant does not try his Lord, but it is God who tries His servant.'" This silenced him.[222] Another story is that the Devil appeared to Jesus once when he was lying down on the ground to sleep, resting his head upon a rock. He asked him how he could possibly have allowed himself to depend on something from this world. In answer, Jesus took the rock from underneath his head and threw it at him.[223]

According to Christian tradition, Jesus was tempted many times by the Devil. First, he fasted for forty days and nights, until he was hungry. Then Satan came to him, challenging him to turn rocks into bread. When this failed to work, he challenged him to throw himself from the top of the temple. Here the Devil's ruse was to challenge his trust in God. He told Jesus to trust in God to command His angels to receive him and break his fall. After Jesus saw through it, the Devil finally took him to a very high mountain, and showed him all the kingdoms of the world and their glory, and said to him, "All these I will give you, if you will fall down and worship me." Then Jesus said to him, "Begone, Satan! For it is written, 'You shall worship the Lord your God and Him alone shall you serve.'"[224]

THE PROPHET ﷺ SEEING THE OTHER DEVILS

That the Prophet ﷺ saw the devils in his vicinity at all times is demonstrated by *ḥadīth*s such as the following. Before leading the Companions in prayer, the Prophet ﷺ said, "*Straighten your ranks, close them, and align your necks, for by He in Whose Hand is my soul, I see the devils penetrating the ranks as if they were small goats.*"[225] He ﷺ also said, "*A demon among devils strongly came at me to interrupt my prayer, but God gave me the upper hand over him. I wished to tie him to one of the pillars of the mosque until morning, so that you all might see him, but then I recalled the words of my brother Solomon,* ***Grant me a kingdom that may not be given to anyone after me.***"[226]

These two *ḥadīth*s describe events occurring in the mosque. In the second the Prophet ﷺ refrains from tying the devil to a palm trunk out of courtesy for a previous Prophet of God, Solomon, whom he calls his brother. Solomon had asked for open mastery over the jinn and had been granted it. He made them work for him, erect buildings, make statues, and manufacture great cooking pots. But he had also asked that this kind of open mastery should remain his exclusive prerogative, a request such as can be made by a Divine Prophet, aware that God loved him and would willingly answer his every request.

The Prophet ﷺ recounted how he had seen the devils in the subtle dimension. He said, "*On the night I was made to travel, we reached the Seventh Heaven and I looked up and saw thunder, lightning and thunderbolts. When I came down to the Terrestrial Heaven I saw clouds of dust, smoke and noise. I asked, 'What is it, O Gabriel?' He replied, 'These are the devils surrounding the eyes of the Children of Adam so that they should not reflect on the Kingdom of the Heavens and the Earth; otherwise they would have seen wonders.'*"[227] We learn from this that the devils blind the eyes of humans from the wonders of the universe, making them forget that these wonders are pointers indicating the Creator Whom they are never supposed to forget. We also learn that had they been attentive to their Lord, they would have seen more wonders, for God would have allowed them greater glimpses into the invisible subtle dimensions.

On another occasion, the Prophet ﷺ described how he was witnessing another kind of habitual interference of the devils with human beings. He said, "*The Devil has his trunk in the heart of the Son of Adam. When the latter remembers [God], he retreats; and when he forgets [Him], he gobbles it.*"[228]

DEVILS BEING AFRAID OF 'UMAR IBN AL-KHAṬṬĀB

The Companions also saw the devils. The Prophet ﷺ was heard saying to 'Umar that no devil ever sees him taking a path without taking another. Clearly, devils avoided 'Umar not only because they knew that his spiritual power and determination were perilous to them, but also that he was able to see them so as to be able to exercise this power.[229]

ABŪ HURAYRA SEEING A DEVIL

As the Companion Abū Hurayra was standing guard for the Prophet ﷺ over the *zakāt* of Ramaḍān, someone came and began to scoop the food up. He seized him, threatening to take him to the Prophet ﷺ. However, as he pleaded that he was in dire need and had a family, Abū Hurayra eventually relented and let him go. In the morning, the Prophet ﷺ asked him, "*Abū Hurayra, what has your captive done last night?*" He answered that he had complained that he was in dire need and had a family, so he felt sorry for him and let him go. The Prophet ﷺ told him that he had lied to him and was sure to return. Being sure that he would return, the Companion kept watch for him. When he reappeared and began to steal food, Abū Hurayra seized him, saying he would take him to the Prophet ﷺ. Again he pleaded so fervently that he succeeded in making Abū Hurayra feel sorry enough to let him go. Once more the Prophet ﷺ asked him, "*Abū Hurayra, what has your captive done last night?*" He ﷺ then reiterated to Abū Hurayra that the miscreant had lied and was sure to return. When caught the third time, the man told Abū Hurayra, "Let me teach you a few words that God will make of benefit to you." He then told him that whenever he was about to go to bed he should recite *Āyat al-Kursī* (the Verse of the Pedestal) and that this would protect him from all devils until morning. When informed of this, the Prophet ﷺ told Abū Hurayra, "*He has told you the truth although he is a liar. Do you know whom you have been talking to for three nights, Abū Hurayra? A devil.*"[230]

SATAN APPEARING TO THE PAGANS OF QURAYSH IN HUMAN FORM

Not only did the Companions see the Devil, but the pagans also saw him in human form. As the leaders of Quraysh were gathering to deliberate about how to best put an end to the Prophet's call in Makka, Satan himself joined them in the guise of a venerable man from Najd. He listened to their suggestions, then pointed out the weaknesses in each of them. But when Abū Jahl suggested that they choose a strong young man from each clan to form a party to assassinate the Prophet ﷺ in his bed, he approved emphatically.[231] The Devil again appeared in Makka in the form of Surāqa, a leader of the Banī Mudlij Clan of the Tribe of Kināna, encouraging the Quraysh to go out to fight the Muslims at Badr, promising them that he would be there to prevent Kināna, with whom they were engaged in a vendetta, from attacking their homes while they were away. He reappeared in the same form on the battlefield, accompanied by his troops, in the form of men of the Banī Mudlij, their banner raised, urging the pagans on. Only when he saw Gabriel charging him did he flee. He kept fleeing until he reached the seashore.[232]

BELIEVERS SEEING THE JINN AND THE DEVILS

Imām Junayd said he once saw Iblīs walking in the market naked, eating a piece of bread. He asked him, "Do you feel no shame, being seen like this?" He replied, "O Abu'l-Qāsim, is there anyone on earth today before whom one should be ashamed? Those before whom one should be ashamed are all under the dust."[233]

Shaykh ʿAbd al-Qādir al-Jīlānī said that in his beginnings, during the days of strenuous striving, he used to see the devils assaulting him in various frightening forms. God, however, gave him the strength to fight and repulse them. Later on he began to see the chief devil Satan himself. He came to him once in the form of a repulsive evil-smelling man, saying, "I am Satan and I have come to serve you, for you have exhausted me and my troops." He said to him, "Away with you! I do not believe you." And the story goes on as one satanic ploy follows another.[234]

Shaykh ʿAlī al-ʿAyyāshī was a man engaged in constant remembrance, hardly ever sleeping, and he was known to be able to see the Devil and beat him with his staff. One day he told him, "I do not fear the staff, but I fear the light of the heart." Shaykh ʿAbd al-Wahhāb says, "One night he sat with us in our gathering devoted to invocations of blessings upon the Prophet ﷺ on Thursday night. Suddenly he picked up his staff and began to beat a man with it. When he asked him why he was beating him, he replied that he was not beating him, but the devil he saw riding on his neck, its two feet dangling on his chest. The spirits of departed saints visited him often, especially Imām Shāfiʿī, and he informed those with him at the time that he saw the Imām in his waking state, not in his dreams. Many who had no idea of his spiritual state thought he was mad."[235]

Again, when the famine at the end of time caused by drought will occur, causing the animals to die of hunger and thirst, the Dajjāl shall tell the Bedouin, "Were I to resurrect your dead camels and you see them come, fat and full of milk, will you know that I am your Lord?" They will acquiesce, upon which he will order the devils to appear to them in the form of their camels. He will ask others, "Were I to resurrect your father, your son and other well-known members of your family for you, will you know that I am your Lord?" Then the devils will appear to them in their guise, seeing which they will follow him.[236]

7
Similitudes in the Higher Worlds

Once the Prophet ﷺ asked Ubayy ibn Kaʿb which verse of the Book of God was greatest and, as already mentioned, he reluctantly answered that he thought it was *Āyat al-Kursī*. The Prophet ﷺ swore that it had two lips and a tongue that glorified the Divine King near the foot of the Throne.[237] Now we know that neither in the physical world nor in the world of the imagination does the Verse of the Pedestal have lips or tongue, so those described by the Prophet ﷺ can therefore only be of the World of Similitudes, where meanings take on subtle forms, and he was able to see and hear this even as it happened in the vicinity of the Divine Throne.

The Prophet ﷺ also told his Companions that their invocations – their *tasbīḥ*, *tahlīl* or *taḥmīd*[i] – circle in procession around the Divine Throne. They make a bee-like humming sound as they keep mentioning the names of those who uttered them in the presence of their Lord.[238]

The authenticated reports in Bukhārī, Muslim and other books of *ḥadīth* state that the Prophet ﷺ said that he was shown in the Seventh Heaven the Populous House, and that Gabriel had informed him that it is visited every day by seventy thousand angels who pray in it, then leave it, never to return.[239] We have to go to weaker transmissions for more details about what the angels do when they leave the House in the Seventh Heaven and about the other parallel Houses in the superimposed dimensions. The following two *ḥadīth*s are from Azraqī, but there are many similar ones from other books of *ḥadīth*, each of which taken individually would be considered weak with regard to its chain of transmission, but collectively would be stronger in view of their numer-

---

i *Tasbīḥ* is to say "*Subḥān Allāh*" (transcendent is God!). *Tahlīl* is to say "*Lā ilāha illa'llāh*" (there is no god other than God), which is the glorification that ascribes Divinity to the One Unique God. *Taḥmīd* is to say "*Al-ḥamdu li'llāh*" (all praise belongs to God).

ous chains of transmission. For when the same *ḥadīth* is transmitted through several different chains, they are considered to strengthen each other, so that the *ḥadīth* may be classified as strong.

The Prophet ﷺ said about the Kaʿba that it was the fifth in a series of fifteen houses, seven of which were in the heavens and seven in the seven earths. The highest he said was the one in proximity to the Throne called the Populous House. Each house has a sacred area surrounding it similar to that of the Kaʿba's. They are superimposed or parallel to each other, so that if a stone were to fall it would land on the next one down, all the way down to the lowest earth. Each of these houses is populated or visited by its people just as the Kaʿba is.[240] He ﷺ also said that it was called the Populous House because it is visited every day by seventy thousand angels who pray in it, then in the evening they descend to circumambulate the Kaʿba, then they visit the Prophet ﷺ in Madina to salute him, after which they leave. Their turn to do this does not return until the Hour.[241]

8
The Speech of Created Beings Not Endowed with Speech

THE SPEECH OF NEWBORN BABIES

Now to move on to another manifestation of *'Ālam al-Mithāl*, the Qur'ān describes how Jesus was able to speak as a newborn baby to defend his mother, who had been falsely accused: ***She pointed to him. They said, "How can we speak to one still in the cradle, a little child?" He said, "I am God's servant. He gave me the Book and made me a Prophet, and made me blessed wherever I may be; and enjoined me to pray and give the poor due so long as I live; and to be loyal to my mother; and He has not made me a wretched tyrant. May peace be upon me the day I was born, the day I die, and the day I am raised up alive."***[242] In addition, the Prophet ﷺ has narrated the stories of two newborns other than Jesus who have spoken in the cradle.[243]

THE SPEECH OF ANIMALS

Once in Madina, the Prophet ﷺ entered a palm grove where there was a camel that moaned and wept as soon as it saw him. The Prophet ﷺ approached and caressed it until it calmed down. Then he asked, "*Who is the master of this camel?*" A young man of the Anṣār came forward saying, "He is mine, O Messenger of God." At which he said to him, "*Will you not fear God in what concerns this animal that He has given you? He has complained to me that you starve and exhaust him.*"[244] Here the camel speaks to the Prophet ﷺ, who understands him perfectly. He has to interpret the camel's speech as no one else is capable of understanding what it says.

A Bedouin of the Banī Sulaym once caught one of the iguana-like lizards of the desert and carried it in his sleeve, intending to roast and eat it as the Bedouin of that region usually did. He came upon the Prophet ﷺ in the midst of a crowd of his Companions, and approached them as he was curious to know what they were about. He inquired what was happening and they told him that this was the man who claimed to be a prophet. He pushed through the crowd until he reached him, and, swearing by his gods, al-Lāt and al-ʿUzzā, said the Prophet ﷺ was more loathsome to him than any other born of a woman and that were he not wary that his own people would accuse him of rashness he would have killed him there and then, thereby gladdening the hearts of everyone. ʿUmar asked for the Prophet's permission to kill him, but was told, "*O ʿUmar, do you not know that he who is gentle comes near to being a prophet?*" Then the Prophet ﷺ turned to the Bedouin saying, "*What made you say what you said, uttering something untrue and showing disrespect to me in the midst of my company?*" The latter retorted mockingly, "And you speak to me too? By al-Lāt and al-ʿUzzā, I shall never believe in you unless this lizard does!" Then, taking the lizard out of his sleeve, he threw it before the Prophet ﷺ. To his amazement, the Prophet ﷺ spoke to the lizard, who answered in a clear Arabic speech that everyone could hear. He asked him whom he worshipped and was answered that it was the Lord of the heavens and the earth. Then he asked him who he was? The lizard answered that he was the Messenger of the Lord of all beings. Astounded, the Bedouin exclaimed, "By God! When I came here, there was none on earth more hateful to me than you, but I now love you more than my father, my eyesight or me. I love you both inwardly and outwardly, with what I show and what I hide. I bear witness that there is no god save God and that you are the Messenger of God."[245] Yet another reported story is that of a gazelle that once spoke to the Prophet ﷺ.[246] In these stories not only the Prophet ﷺ understands the speech of the lizard and the gazelle, but those around him can also hear these animals speak in clear Arabic and understand them. The phenomenon may conceivably be attributed to the blessed presence of the Prophet ﷺ.

However, the Prophet ﷺ recounted similar stories – where no divine envoy was there – of ordinary people from previous nations. He ﷺ said,

"A man who was once driving a cow decided to ride her instead, at which she turned to him saying, 'We have not been created for this; we have only been created for tillage.'" The Companions around him exclaimed, "*Subḥān Allāh*!"[i] He ﷺ said, *"I believe this, as do Abū Bakr and 'Umar,"* his two close Companions who were not there at the time. Then he ﷺ continued, *"A man was once with his sheep, when a wolf carried away one of them. The shepherd pursued him, so he let it go, saying, 'How will it be when they have no other shepherd but me?'"* Again, the Companions exclaimed, "*Subḥān Allāh*!" Once more, he ﷺ said, *"I believe this, as do Abū Bakr and 'Umar,"* who were still absent.[247] In these two stories a cow and a wolf speak in an intelligible manner, which is manifestly impossible were they to use their vocal cords. Therefore, something else is at play here, a mechanism external to the material world but that interacts with it, whereby thoughts are vocalised and heard in a manner different from the norm. Here neither the Prophet ﷺ nor any other blessed person are present, so that the phenomenon cannot be attributed such a spiritual influence.

We thus learn that people other than Divine Prophets can have such experiences; and indeed, we find similar episodes in the lives of the Companions of the Prophet ﷺ and other men of God. For instance, Safīna, the Prophet's servant, recounted that he had once met a lion in a wood. When he saw it heading towards him, he spoke to it, simply stating that he was Safīna, the Prophet's servant. That was obviously sufficient, for the lion rubbed his shoulder against him, walked with him until he reached the road, then growled at him, which the Companion took as bidding him farewell.[248]

'Uqba ibn Nāfi', who was born during the Prophet's lifetime yet never met him and is therefore not considered to be a Companion but a Follower, commanded an army during the conquest of North Africa. He founded the city of Qayrawān, choosing a valley full of trees and bushes that also had various carnivores and snakes. It was reported that he cried out three times, "We are settling here, therefore depart!" Consequently, the reptiles and beasts of the valley took their young and

---

i The use of *"Subḥān Allāh!"* in such a context is an exclamation of astonishment at something being awesome or wonderful.

departed. He then said to his people, "Move in, in the Name of God." He ordered the trees cut down and burnt, and built the city at the location where it stands today.[249]

One of the biographers of Shaykh ʿAbd al-Qādir al-Jīlānī reports him as recounting that once, as a child in his hometown, he went out into the fields on the Day of ʿArafāt, the day that represents the pinnacle of the pilgrimage's rites, when the pilgrims gather together on the plain of ʿArafāt near Makka. For a while he followed a ploughing cow, when suddenly the cow turned to him and said, "This is not what you were created for, O ʿAbd al-Qādir!" He rushed home in a fright, climbed up onto the roof and, to his surprise, was able to see the pilgrims on ʿArafāt from his house in Central Asia. Even as a child, these events made him realise that his spiritual state was exceptional, so he asked for his mother's permission to leave for Baghdad, the capital of the eastern Islamic world at the time, to acquire the religious sciences from the scholars and follow the spiritual path with its masters.[250]

THE SPEECH OF BIRDS AND INSECTS

There is mention in the Qur'ān of birds and insects speaking, while the Prophet ﷺ spoke of many other animals. The Qur'ān says, ***And Solomon was David's heir. He said, "O people, we have been taught the speech of the birds; we have been given of everything; this, indeed, is the clear favour." And his hosts were mustered to Solomon, jinn, men and birds, one group following another; till, when they came to the Valley of the Ants, an ant said, "Ants, enter your houses, lest Solomon and his hosts crush you unaware!" He smiled, laughing at its words, and said, "My Lord, inspire me to thank for Your blessings with which You have blessed me and my parents and to work the deeds that please You, and make me by Your mercy among Your virtuous servants."*** Having stated that Solomon (Sulaymān) could understand the speech of the birds and hear and understand ants communicating with each other, the Qur'ān then goes on to describe an extraordinary conversation taking place between him and the hoopoe.[251] Such occurrences can only be explained by reference to the properties of the *ʿĀlam al-Mithāl*, for how else in the physical world could insects and birds make themselves understood to man. However, only those men (like Solomon) who are in possession of a high degree of spirituality are capable of perceiving such things, each according to their rank, for not every part of the *ʿĀlam al-Mithāl* is perceptible to every man of God. Yet it may be that a man of lesser calibre will witness realities that are hidden from a more spiritual one.

As Shaykh Yāqūt al-ʿArshī was sitting amidst his disciples, a pigeon alighted on his shoulder and seemed to whisper something in his ear. He said, "*Bismi'llāh* [In the Name of God], we shall send one of the disciples with you." It said, "Only you will do for me." He then rode from Alexandria to Cairo on his mule, entered ʿAmr's Mosque and asked to meet the muezzin whom he asked for by name. When he came, the Shaykh told him that this pigeon had informed him in Alexandria that each time her eggs hatched where she had laid them in the minaret he took her chicks and killed them. The man answered, "She has spoken truly; I have taken them many times." The Shaykh said, "Do not do it again." He replied, "I repent to God – exalted is He!" Upon hearing this, the Shaykh returned to Alexandria.[252]

THE SPEECH OF TREES AND INANIMATE THINGS

We also find that there is not only life but also consciousness in trees and what is generally considered to be inanimate matter.

ʿAlī recounted that, when he walked with the Prophet ﷺ around Makka, there was scarcely' a hill or a tree they passed by that did not greet him, saying, "May peace be upon you, O Messenger of God!"[253] The Prophet ﷺ himself said, "*I know a certain stone in Makka that used to greet me with salām before I became a Prophet.*"[254]

Once, as he was in the outskirts of Makka in the Ḥajūn neighbourhood,[i] heavy-hearted because he had been ill-treated by his fellow Makkans, Gabriel came to the Prophet ﷺ. According to one version of the story he asked him, "Would you like me to show you a sign?" According to another account, the Prophet ﷺ had asked his Lord, "*O God, show me a sign today such that I shall no longer care who gives me the*

i The Ḥajūn neighbourhood is near the Maʿlā Cemetery, north of old Makka, but now part of the city.

lie." Both versions then go on to state that Gabriel said to him, "Call this tree." The Prophet ﷺ called it and it rushed towards him, furrowing the ground, until it stood before him and greeted him with salām. "Tell it to go back," said Gabriel. The Prophet ﷺ did so, then according to one version he said, "*I shall never care, after this, who of my people shall give me the lie.*" Or, according to the other version, "*I have seen enough.*"[255] In this incident, we see a tree hearing the Prophet's summons and obeying it, even though it possesses neither ears to hear nor legs to move. Both qualities require the intervention of a non-materialistic dimension that allows for such phenomena and interacts with sufficient intimacy with the material dimension to make them appear there.

Numerous Companions witnessed and related the following story. The Prophet ﷺ used to lean on a palm trunk in his mosque as he delivered his Friday sermons. When they made a pulpit of three steps for him and he climbed it for the first time, the trunk began to wail in anguish. Everyone there could hear it clearly and testified that it continued to do so until the Prophet ﷺ placed his hand on it and embraced it, and only then did it stop.[256] Here the living tree of the previous story is replaced with a dead trunk, which was to all appearances inanimate. Other inanimate things such as food, wood and a rocky mountain exhibit similar phenomena in the following stories.

During the campaign of Khaybar, the Prophet ﷺ sat down to eat with his Companions. The meal was roasted mutton offered to them by a Jewish woman. The Prophet ﷺ picked up the shoulder and ate a piece, and so did his Companions. Then he said, "*Eat no more.*" Then he sent for the Jewish woman to ask her, "*Did you poison this sheep?*" "Who informed you?" she retorted. "*This,*" he said, showing her the shoulder in his hand. "Yes, I did," she said. "*Why did you do it?*" he asked. She replied that she had thought that if he was indeed a Prophet, it would not harm him, but if he was not, then they would be rid of him.[257]

The Prophet ﷺ once visited his uncle ʿAbbās in his home, and asked him and his sons to come close together. He covered them with a sheet, then said, "*My Lord, this is my uncle, my father's brother, and these are the people of my house, veil them from the Fire just as I have covered them with this sheet of mine!*" At this, the door frame and the walls of the house were heard to repeat, "Amen! Amen! Amen!"[258]

THE SPEECH OF CREATED BEINGS NOT ENDOWED WITH SPEECH

The Prophet ﷺ, Abū Bakr, ʿUmar and ʿUthmān once climbed Mount Uḥud. The mountain trembled beneath them, so the Prophet ﷺ stamped on it, saying, "*Stand still, Uḥud! There is upon you only a Prophet, a Ṣiddīq, and two martyrs.*"[259] Mount Uḥud is shown here to possess awareness, for it trembled with joy at the proximity of the Prophet ﷺ and his Companions, and the Prophet ﷺ confirmed this by addressing it in the same manner that one addresses a sentient being.

ALL CREATED BEINGS GLORIFY THEIR LORD

We have seen how living beings as well as inanimate matter show evidence of life and consciousness of a kind that would remain entirely unsuspected were one to confine one's observation to the external appearance of things. Another very important manifestation of life and consciousness is that, as we are told in the Qur'ān, the entire universe hymns the praises of its Creator, but in a manner that is not perceptible to the physical senses. Muslim scholars have explained that everything in creation has two faces: one turned towards God and the other towards creation. The first is the one that by its very nature constantly glorifies its Maker, while the glorification of the second is voluntary and exclusive to sentient beings. Thus the latter, humans and jinn – even the disbelievers among them – and angels, share with all other creatures the inward form of innate glorification, but not the optional outward kind. When the Qur'ān says, ***The seven heavens and the earth glorify Him and everyone in them glorifies Him. There is nothing that does not extol His praise, but you do not understand their praises. He is Forbearing, Forgiving,***[260] the reference is to the first kind of glorification, the one shared by both sentient and non-sentient creatures, including inanimate things. While His saying, ***Have you not seen how God is glorified by everyone in the heavens and the earth, and the birds which spread their wings? Each knows his prayers and his praises; and God knows what they do,***[261] refers to both, as prayers are for sentient beings, whilst glorification in general is shared by all others.

We now come to incidents involving the glorification of trees, mountains, and other inanimate objects. The Qur'ān says, ***And We granted David of Our favour; "O mountains, echo with him!" and***

the birds.[262] We are given to know from this verse that when Prophet David hymned his praises to God, which became known as the Psalms, the mountains around him hymned them echoing him and so did the birds.

Abū Dharr al-Ghifārī said, "I was sitting in the Prophet's circle and there were pebbles in his hand. These pebbles were glorifying God in his palm, so that everyone in the circle could hear them. He handed them over to Abū Bakr and they were heard to glorify. Then Abū Bakr gave them back. The Prophet ﷺ handed them over to ʿUmar, and they were heard to glorify. The latter gave them back and they were handed over to ʿUthmān. The same thing happened. Then he gave them to us and they glorified with none of us."[263]

ʿAbdallāh ibn Masʿūd described how they used to hear the food glorifying God as they ate with the Prophet ﷺ.[264]

Before becoming a great Sufi, Ibrāhīm ibn Adham was a prince. One day, as he was hunting in the wilderness around the city of Balkh, he heard a voice saying, "Ibrāhīm! Is this what you were created for? Is this what you were ordered to do?" Then again, a while later, he was addressed from the pommel of his saddle, "By God! This is not what you were created for, nor is it what you were ordered to do!" This time he dismounted, and seeing one of his father's shepherds, he gave him his horse and his clothes, took his woollen tunic, and walked away into the desert to begin a life of asceticism.[265]

The late Shaykh Muḥammad Mubārak often recounted to us how one of his spiritual masters, Shaykh Aḥmad Riḍwān, went through a period as a young man when he could not bring himself to pass water in the desert, for he heard the sand and pebbles glorifying God. In distress, he asked God to veil this from him. I have come across numerous similar occurrences recorded in the lives of great men of God.

9
Interactions between the World of the Dead and the World of the Living

HEARING THE VOICES OF THE DEAD

Hearing the speech of the dead, yet another manifestation of the *'Ālam al-Mithāl*, could have been mentioned in the previous chapter, for we know that the dead have no apparatus with which to produce a voice. Their speech could very well have been classified under the same heading as the speech of all other creatures incapable of speaking in the ordinary manner. However, it seemed more appropriate to discuss it in the context of the interaction between the worlds of the living and the dead.

Hearing the speech of the dead has been abundantly reported from the Prophet's time until today. The Prophet ﷺ once heard the voices of two men being punished in their graves and said, "*They are being punished, and not for anything very great. One of them was not careful with his urine, while the other used to spread gossip among the people.*" Then he asked for a palm branch, broke it in two, and placed half of it on each grave. They asked him why he had done this and he ﷺ answered, "*It may be that this would relieve them a little, so long as it [the branch] has not become dry.*"[266] On at least three occasions when the Prophet ﷺ was walking with Bilāl – twice in the Baqī' Cemetery and a third time in a garden of Abū Ṭalḥa's – they passed by a grave and the Prophet ﷺ asked Bilāl if he could hear what he heard. When Bilāl answered that he could not, the Prophet ﷺ said that he could hear those entombed in those graves being tormented.[267] Another Companion, Abū Rāfi', reported that the Prophet ﷺ went out in the middle of the night to pray for the dead in the Baqī' Cemetery. As he was walking back after finishing, and passed by a certain grave, he said, "*Uff, uff!*" Worried that he might have done something to annoy him, for there was nobody else around, Abū Rāfiʿ asked the Prophet ﷺ why he had done this and he answered that it was because a man in a grave had been questioned about the Prophet ﷺ and had been found to doubt him.[268]

Al-ʿUtbī said, "I was sitting before the Prophet's tomb when a Bedouin arrived and said, 'May peace be upon you, O Messenger of God. I have heard God say, ***Were they, when they wrong themselves, to come to you and ask God for forgiveness, and were the Messenger to ask forgiveness for them, they would find God Relenting, Compassionate.***[269] I have come to you seeking forgiveness for my sins, seeking your influence (*jāh*) with my Lord.'" Then, according to ʿUtbī, the Bedouin recited a few verses of poetry. These have since been inscribed on the two pillars flanking the brass grill before the Prophet's tomb. "The Bedouin departed," continued ʿUtbī, "and I was overcome by somnolence, wherein I saw the Prophet ﷺ saying, '*Follow the Bedouin, O ʿUtbī, and convey to him the glad news that God has indeed forgiven him.*'"[270]

The Prophet ﷺ said, "*No man ever passes by the grave of another he used to know in this world ,and greets him with salām, except that he will know him and return his salām.*"[271] Furthermore, Abū Hurayra said, "When a man passes by the grave of another whom he used to know and greets him with *salām*, he recognises him and returns his *salām*; when it is one whom he did not know and who does not recognise him, he still returns his *salām*."[272]

The Prophet ﷺ also said, "*Were it not for the fear that you would no longer bury each other, I would have prayed to God to make you hear the torment of the grave.*"[273] On many occasions, the Prophet ﷺ informed his Companions that he saw and heard people being tormented in their graves. Now if these graves were to be opened, nothing would appear to the physical eye save bodies decaying in sandy pits or the bones. What the inner eye witnesses, however, is quite different. He once informed them, as he passed near a Jewish graveyard, that he heard Jews being tormented in their graves.[274]

ʿUmar ibn al-Khaṭṭāb once addressed the dead in the Baqīʿ Cemetery of Madina: "May peace be upon you, O people of the graves! Our news is that your women have remarried, your houses have been occupied, and your money has been divided." A voice answered him, "O ʿUmar ibn al-Khaṭṭāb, our news is that what we sent ahead we found, what we spent we have won, and what we have left behind we lost."[275]

The Companion Ṭalḥa ibn ʿUbayd Allāh said that one day he had gone to look at his land in the region north of Madina known as al-Ghāba, and, when night fell, he sat near the grave of ʿAbdallāh ibn ʿAmr ibn Ḥarām, one of the martyrs of the Battle of Uḥud, and he heard melodious Qur'ān recitation coming from the grave, more beautiful than anything he had heard before. He reported this to the Prophet ﷺ who told him that it had been ʿAbdallāh.[276]

Ibn ʿAbbās said that one of the Prophet's Companions once unknowingly pitched his tent on top of a grave, and heard a human voice reciting *Sūra al-Mulk* from beginning to end. The moment he met the Prophet ﷺ he told him, "O Messenger of God, I struck my tent on a grave, unaware that it was there, and I heard a man reciting *Sūra Tabārak al-Mulk* until he completed it." The Prophet ﷺ answered him, "*It is a guardian, a saviour: it will save him from the torment of the grave.*"[277]

Khālid ibn Maʿdān, a well-known pious Follower, is reported to have said that *Sūra al-Sajda* defends the grave's occupant, pleading, "O God, if I am part of Your Book, then allow me to intercede on his behalf, and if I am not, then erase me from it." He added that it becomes like a bird spreading its wings over him, interceding for him, and preventing the torment of the grave from reaching him. The same goes for *Sūra Tabārak* and Khālid ibn Maʿdān never went to sleep without reciting them.[278]

It has been reported that, during his caliphate, ʿUmar ibn al-Khaṭṭāb once spoke to a young man who had died and been buried the night before. He called him by his name and said to him, "To him who fears the rank of his Lord shall be two gardens." The youth answered from his grave, "O ʿUmar, God has given them to me in Paradise, twice over."[279]

A saintly woman Tahallul bint al-ʿIṭaf often visited the martyrs of Uḥud. She said, "I once rode to visit them and prayed for a while near the grave of Ḥamza, the son of ʿAbd al-Muṭṭalib. When I was done I rose to my feet and waved my hand at them in salute, and I heard clearly with my ears a greeting coming from underneath the ground.

I recognised it [as clearly] as I recognise that God created me and [as clearly as I can distinguish] night from day. There was no one else in the valley, neither someone uttering prayers, nor answering, save my servant boy who had fallen asleep, while holding the bridle of my mount. I felt every hair on me bristle and I immediately summoned the boy to bring my mount, which he did and I rode home."[280]

Yazīd al-Bajlī said that after his brother died and was buried he placed his head on his grave, his left ear to the ground, and heard his brother's voice faintly saying, "Allāh!" Then his brother was asked, "What then is your religion?" And he answered, "Islām."[281]

Sayyid ʿAbd al-Raḥmān ibn al-Shaykh ʿAlī Bā-ʿAlawī[i] used to say that, whenever he visited the grave of his ancestor al-Faqīh al-Muqaddam at the cemetery of Tarīm and was reciting verses from the Qur'ān and made some error or forgot a verse, he heard the voice of al-Faqīh from the grave correcting him. He also said that he heard the voice of his own father saying from the grave, "Go from the sun." He once sat at the side of the grave of one of his companions wishing to prompt him to say, "*Lā ilāha illa'llāh*," but then rose having said nothing. When asked, he answered that he had seen his uncle ʿAbdallāh with the dead person, saying, "He needs no prompting."[282] These occurrences were quite frequent in the life of the *Sayyid* and were regarded as not particularly extraordinary.

A vast number of such occurrences were reported by Imām ʿAbd al-Wahhāb al-Shaʿrānī, the Egyptian scholar and saint from the tenth century of the Hijra, in his well-known compilation of biographies entitled *al-Ṭabaqāt al-Kubrā*, among which are the following.

Shaykh ʿAlī al-ʿAyyāshī slept one night in the *zāwiya* of Imām ʿAbd al-Wahhāb al-Shaʿrānī's dead grandfather, Shaykh ʿAlī al-Shaʿrānī, and heard him reciting the Qur'ān all night, starting with *Sūra Maryam* and ending with *Sūra al-Raḥmān* with the break of dawn, at which time the voice faded away. He mentioned this to the people of the village, only to find them already familiar with the phenomenon, for they

---

i *Sayyid* ʿAbd al-Raḥmān son of the illustrious Shaykh ʿAlī , son of Shaykh Abū Bakr al-Sakrān, son of Imām ʿAbd al-Raḥmān al-Saqqāf. Great Ḥaḍramī saint of the 10th century AH.

immediately said, "This is Shaykh ʿAlī, may God have mercy on him."[283]

Shaykh ʿAlī al-Khawwāṣ al-Burullusī, another of Shaʿrānī's masters, said, "Contrary to the shaykhs of the jurists (*fuqahā'*), the shaykhs of the people [or *qawm,* as the Sufis are commonly known] answer their disciples (*fuqarā'*) from their graves only because they sincerely believe in their shaykhs, but not so the students of the scholars. Should the jurist (*faqīh*) be sincere, Imām Shāfiʿī would answer him and speak to him."[284]

When Shaykh Muḥammad al-Ḥanafī visited the cemetery and greeted the dead with *salām* in their graves, they greeted him back in a manner that could be heard by those accompanying him.[285]

Shaykh Amīn al-Dīn, imām of the Ghamrī Mosque, informed Imām ʿAbd al-Wahhāb that a man buried in the graveyard was heard screaming from sunset to sunrise every night. This was reported to Shaykh Muḥammad ibn ʿAnān, who went to the grave, recited *Sūra Tabārak* and prayed to God to forgive him. Thereafter, no screaming was heard from that grave.[286]

Imām ʿAbd al-Wahhāb al-Shaʿrānī says that when he visited *Sayyid* Aḥmad al-Badawī in the company of one of his closest masters, Shaykh Muḥammad al-Shinnāwī, he heard the latter speak to him and *Sayyid* Aḥmad al-Badawī answer him.[287] On one of these occasions, Shaykh al-Shinnāwī asked *Sayyid* Aḥmad al-Badawī his opinion as to whether he should undertake a certain journey. He heard him answer him, "Go and rely on God." On recounting the episode, he specified that he had heard this with his ears.[288]

Many other people reported over the years hearing the voices of *Sayyid* Aḥmad al-Badawī addressing them. Shaykh Aḥmad Ḥijāb, for instance, who died in the 1970s, wrote that, after his first spiritual master died in Ṭanṭā, Egypt, he became a disciple of *Sayyid* Aḥmad al-Badawī and often heard him teaching and instructing him. *Sayyid* al-Badawī used to command him firmly, "Silence! Silence!" when he had in fact been silent. He realised, then, that he was being instructed to stop the incidental trivial thoughts in his head and resume his attentiveness to God. At other times, *Sayyid* al-Badawī commanded him to remember and invoke God. Sometimes when there was a question preoccupying him, the *Sayyid* answered it. He notes with surprise that he heard the answer but not the question that had been formulated in his own mind, for the answer was a voice in his ear, while the question had been just a thought.[289]

A Bā-ʿAlawī *sayyid* recounted that he once visited the cemetery at night in the company of Imām ʿAbdallāh al-Ḥaddād. He had some sweet basil in his hand. When they reached the grave of al-Faqīh al-Muqaddam, the Imām asked him to place some of it on his grave and the rest on the grave of his own wife Khadīja. "I do not know which grave is hers," he replied. The Imām said, "Head toward the grave of Shaykh ʿUmar al-Meḥḍār and you shall find it." When the *sayyid* approached the grave of Shaykh ʿUmar al-Meḥḍār he heard a voice repeating, "My grave is here, my grave is here!" He followed the voice until he reached the place it came from, placed the rest of the aromatic herb on it, and rushed back to the Imām quite frightened.[290] In this story we can see how the Imām knew beforehand by unveiling that his late wife would be aware of their visit and able to call his companion and direct him to her grave, and how the latter was able to hear clearly the voice of a dead person, which frightened him greatly because he was obviously unaccustomed to such occurrences.

THE DEAD HEAR THE VOICES OF THE LIVING AND ARE AWARE OF WHAT THEY DO

We know from the Prophet ﷺ that he remains aware of the happenings in the lives of every single member of his community after his death. Not only that, but he also informed us that ordinary people will be aware after their deaths of many of the things that happen to their relatives and friends. It seems that the degree of awareness depends on the spiritual level of the person: the more spiritually developed the person, the more aware he will be.

The Prophet ﷺ told us that after his death the works of his community would be presented to him and he will ask forgiveness for the sinners, even before his intercession for them on the Day of Judgement. He ﷺ said, "*My life is good for you: you do things and things are done for you; and my death is good for you: your works are presented to me, and if what I see is good I thank God, and if it is evil I ask forgiveness for you.*"[291]

INTERACTIONS BETWEEN THE WORLD OF THE DEAD AND THE WORLD OF THE LIVING

He also informed us that a dead person perceives the sound of the footsteps of men in a funeral procession. He ﷺ said, "*When the servant is placed in his grave and the people walk away, he hears the sounds of their sandals.*"[292] He ﷺ also said, "*When a man visits the grave of his brother and sits there, the latter rejoices and answers him until he departs.*"[293] And he said, "*No man ever passes by the grave of another that he used to know in this world and greets him with salām without him recognizing him and greeting him back.*"[294]

History tells us that the day after the victory of Badr, the Prophet ﷺ returned to the pit where the pagan chiefs had been buried, stood at the edge, and addressed them saying, "*Have you found God's promises to be true?*"[295] When his Companions asked him how he spoke to men who were already rotting, he answered that they, his Companions, were not more able to hear his voice than those in the ground.

ʿĀṣim al-Jaḥdarī was seen in a dream-vision two years after he died.[i] He was asked, "Where are you now?" He answered, "I and some of my companions visit Abū Bakr al-Muzanī every Thursday night and Friday morning and receive your news." He was asked, "With your bodies or your spirits?" He replied, "The bodies have perished; it is but the spirits that meet." "Are you aware of our visits to you?" "Yes, we are aware of them, especially on Friday evenings and Saturday until sunrise."[296]

THE PROPHET ﷺ ANSWERS THOSE WHO GREET HIM

We know from the above that the Prophet ﷺ is aware of those who visit him and those who invoke blessings upon him. His answers, however, are not heard by everyone. Nevertheless, many masters have reported hearing the Prophet's voice returning their greetings, either when they visit him in Madina, or when they recite the *tashahhud* at the end of their prayers, which includes greeting him with salām. At the end of time, on his second coming, Jesus and those around him will hear the Prophet's answer to his greetings.

The Prophet ﷺ said, "*By He in Whose Hand lies the soul of Abu'l-Qāsim, ʿĪsā, the son of Mary, shall descend, a fair-minded leader and a just judge.*

---

i He was a master of the sciences of Qur'ān recitation and exegesis from Baṣra, and a student of al-Ḥasan al-Baṣrī. He died in 128 AH.

He will break the cross and kill the pig and make concord among the people and remove hostility. He will be offered money but will not accept it. He will stand before my tomb and say, 'O Muḥammad!', and I shall answer him."[297]

Shaykh Muḥammad al-Ḥanafī once saw a man seemingly from a faraway country in the street and remarked, "Whenever this man prays his *fajr* Prayer and invokes blessings on the Prophet ﷺ, he hears him saluting him back, which increases his light until it becomes like the light of day."[298]

It is also on record that when Shaykh Ṣadr al-Dīn al-Bakrī went for *ḥajj*, visited the Prophet ﷺ and greeted him with *salām*, he heard him greeting him back.[299] The same is said of many other masters, among whom is Imām ʿAbdallāh al-Ḥaddād. The latter greeted the Prophet ﷺ when he arrived to Madina and all those who were with him heard the Prophet ﷺ return his greeting. He later recounted the episode in poetry.[300]

Shaykh Aḥmad al-Rifāʿī, who lived in Iraq, visited the Prophet ﷺ in Madina during his *ḥajj* journey. He was accompanied by a thousand disciples. As he stood before the Prophet's tomb, he recited some verses he had composed, the gist of which were that while in Iraq he had sent his spirit to Madina to greet the Prophet ﷺ, but now that he had arrived physically, he was requesting the Prophet ﷺ to extend his hand for him to kiss. The Prophet ﷺ then extended his hand and he kissed it. The event was witnessed by the scores of disciples surrounding him at that time.[301] The thing to notice here is that in all the aforementioned episodes, when the Prophet ﷺ returned the greeting, he was heard by everyone present.

As for those occurrences when only the person concerned hears it, they are literally innumerable. I knew an Indian security guard in Madina who hailed from Mumbai. He confided in me that when he greeted the Prophet ﷺ, he often saw a subtle image of him greeting him back. Again, once when the late Shaykh Muḥammad Mubārak was standing visiting the Prophet ﷺ, Shaykh Maḥmūd, a professor of *Ḥadīth* at the Islamic University in Madina, came and stood next to him. As they walked out of the mosque together, Shaykh Maḥmūd said, "Shaykh Muḥammad, I just saw the Prophet ﷺ saying that you will receive good news shortly." Soon, out of the blue, Shaykh Muḥammad Mubārak was informed by Sharīf Shaḥḥāt that he and his wife were welcome to stay in the old house where Shaykh Abu'l-Wafā al-Sharqāwī had lived during his long sojourn in Madina, not far from the Prophet's Mosque, for as long as they wished. Since his arrival in Madina - where he was to die - Shaykh Mubārak had been staying with his son at some distance from the Mosque. He had found it difficult to travel to and fro daily with his elderly wife. Shaykh Abu'l-Wafā al-Sharqāwī was a great man of God from Egypt, who was one of the masters of Shaykh Aḥmad Riḍwān, Shaykh Mubārak's spiritual master. Thus, Shaykh Mubārak was immensely delighted to find quarters in the house of his master's master. As for the man who made the offer, Sharīf Shaḥḥāt, he was running the estate of Shaykh Abu'l-Wafā al-Sharqāwī, a *waqf* or inalienable property that was run as a charity.

I heard from the same Shaykh Mubārak that one of his former teachers at al-Azhar University, Shaykh Muḥammad Ḥabīb Allāh al-Shinqīṭī, the *muḥaddith*,[i] had just before his death confided in one his closest disciples that when he was living in Madina, he had once stayed behind until they had closed the doors of the Prophet's Mosque at night. When there was no one around, he had gone to stand before the Prophet's tomb and requested that he extend his hand for him to kiss, just as he had done for Shaykh Aḥmad al-Rifā'ī. The Prophet ﷺ then extended his hand and he kissed it, but had kept it a closely-guarded secret until confiding in his disciple.

Once when Ḥabīb ʿUmar ibn Sumayṭ and Ḥabīb Aḥmad Mashhūr al-Ḥaddād were visiting the Prophet ﷺ together, it was noticed by their entourage that Ḥabīb ʿUmar had been greatly affected by the visit. As they stepped out of the mosque he was seen to be weeping. Then he was heard to murmur in Ḥabīb Aḥmad's ear, "Did you hear what he said? Did you hear what he said?" No one dared ask them, neither then nor later, so that is all we know about the event.

---

i Shaykh Muḥammad Ḥabīb Allāh al-Shinqīṭī of Mauritania, master of *Ḥadīth* and other religious sciences, moved from Mauritania to Morocco then to the Ḥijāz, before spending the last years of his life in Cairo where he taught at al-Azhar University. He died in 1363 AH / 1944 CE.

THE PRESENTATION OF WORKS

For the dead to perceive directly what the living are about is one of the modes of perception pertaining to the *'Ālam al-Mithāl*. Another phenomenon is the showing of works. We have already quoted the most important *ḥadīth* where the Prophet ﷺ says, "*My life is good for you: you do things and things are done for you; and my death is good for you: your works are presented to me, and if what I see is good I thank God, and if it is evil I ask forgiveness for you.*"[302] He ﷺ also said, "*Increase your invocations of blessings on me on Fridays, for your invocations are shown to me. He who is most abundant in his invocations of blessings upon me will be nearest to me.*"[303] He ﷺ explained that Friday was the best of all days, calling it the "*radiant day*" and calling the night before the "*radiant night*",[304] and advised his Companions that they should strive to make abundant invocations of blessings upon him on that day, as these invocations would be presented to him. He was asked, "How can they be shown to you, O Messenger of God, after you have decayed?" He answered, "*God has forbidden the bodies of the Prophets to the earth.*"[305] An eminent Follower, Sa'īd ibn al-Musayyab, used to say, "No day passes by without the Prophet ﷺ being shown his community morning and evening and his recognising them by their marks. This is so he should be able to testify on their behalf. God – exalted and blessed is He! – says, ***How, then, shall it be when We bring from each community a witness and bring you to witness against those?*** [306]

It is not only the Prophet ﷺ who is shown the works of his community, but so too are the believers. Five Companions at least – Abū Ayyūb al-Anṣārī, Anas ibn Mālik, Abū Hurayra, Jābir ibn 'Abdallāh and Abu'l-Dardā' – have each reported a different occasion on which the Prophet ﷺ stated that the works of the living were not only shown to him, but to the dead dwelling in the Intermediary World (*Barzakh*), which is usually termed the "grave" in *ḥadīth*.[307] They reported that the Prophet ﷺ said, "*Your works are shown to your dead relatives and tribesmen. When these works are good, they are happy, but when they are not they say, 'O God, let them not die before You guide them as You have guided us.'*"[308] He also said that they should be careful about how they behave, for their works are shown to their brothers in their graves.[309]

INTERACTIONS BETWEEN THE WORLD OF THE DEAD AND THE WORLD OF THE LIVING

For the Companions, the Followers and succeeding generations this was common knowledge. It was taken for granted that it was not only known to the more knowledgeable but to everyone else as well. They often reminded each other of these facts to encourage one another not to stray from the straight path. Abu'l-Dardā', a close friend of ʿAbdallāh ibn Rawāḥa, both of whom were famous Companions, used to say after the latter was martyred at Mu'ta fighting against the Byzantines, "O God, I seek your protection against doing anything that would shame ʿAbdallāh ibn Rawāḥa."[310]

A man of God, ʿAyyād al-Khawwāṣ, visited the governor of Palestine at that time, Ibrāhīm ibn Ṣāliḥ, and the latter said to him, "Counsel me." He said, "What counsel am I to give you? May God improve your condition! It has been reported to me that the works of the living are shown to their dead relatives, so be careful of your works, which will be shown to the Messenger of God ﷺ." Upon hearing this, Ibrāhīm wept until his tears ran down his beard.[311]

Ṣadaqa ibn Sulaymān al-Jaʿfarī said he had been used to behaving in any way he pleased until his father died. Soon afterward he repented and stopped what he had been doing. However, it so happened that one day he relapsed. It was not long before he saw his father in his sleep saying to him, "My son, how happy I was with you and your works that had been shown to us and that we saw resembled those of the men of God! But now I am greatly ashamed. Shame me no more in the sight of the dead persons around me!"[312]

Come Judgement Day, the actions of every single human being will be shown to him,[313] whether good or evil, and his hands, his feet and, as the case may be, other parts of him will testify against him: ***Today We shall seal their mouths and their hands will speak to Us, and their feet will testify as to what they used to earn.***[314]

THE MOMENT OF DEATH

ʿUmar ibn al-Khaṭṭāb said, "Visit the dying and remind them, for they see and hear what you do not. Inculcate the testimony of *Lā ilāha illa'llāh* in them."[315] We know that what ʿUmar meant in saying that the dying see what the living do is that, in detaching themselves from the concerns of this life and in preparation for crossing over to the other side, their souls become liberated from ordinary veils and are capable of witnessing the subtle realities surrounding them. They will see the Angel of Death and other angels, the spirits of those who have died before them, glimpses of Paradise, and so on.

When one of the greatest Companions, Salmān the Persian, visited one of his friends in his last moments, he said, "O Angel of Death, be gentle on him for he is a believer." The dying man said, "He says, 'I am gentle on all believers.'"[316]

Centuries later, when a man renowned for his generosity, al-Ḥakam ibn al-Muṭṭalib al-Makhzūmī, complained in his last moments about how death was severely distressing him, he fainted. A man next to him prayed to God to make it easy on him, adding that he had been exceedingly generous. Shortly thereafter he came to and asked whom it was who had just spoken. They named the man, so he said to him, "The Angel of Death says to you, 'I am gentle on every generous believer,'" and then he expired.[317]

When the time had come for Salmān to die he asked his wife for the musk he had given her for safekeeping. She brought it, saying, "Here it is." He said, "Sprinkle it around me, for there shall come to me creatures of God who neither eat food nor drink, but can perceive fragrance."[318]

Another one of the great Companions, Muʿādh ibn Jabal, died in his early thirties in the epidemic called the Epidemic of Emmaus, which decimated vast regions of Palestine. His son died before him and he showed great fortitude, accepting God's decision to take his son from him. Then one day he noticed that the disease had appeared on his palm, so he kissed it saying, "A beloved one arriving at a time of need, may he who is regretful not succeed." They said to him, "Do you see anything, O Muʿādh?" He said, "Yes, my Lord is rewarding me for my uncomplaining patience. The spirit of my son has come to give me the glad news that Muḥammad is in the midst of a hundred ranks of the angels nearest to God and also the Martyrs and the Virtuous are blessing my soul and waiting to escort me to Paradise." Then he lost consciousness and was seen as if shaking hands with someone and heard saying, "Welcome, welcome, welcome, I am coming to join you."[319] Another Companion, Yazīd ibn Shajara, said, "No dying person passes away without his companions in this life being shown to him, whether they are people of frivolity or people of remembrance."[320]

Yet another Companion, al-Miswar ibn Makhrama, lost consciousness during his terminal illness and when he came to said, "I testify that there no god other than God and that Muḥammad is the Messenger of God. To be connected with God is dearer to me than the whole world and all that it contains. ʿAbd al-Raḥmān ibn ʿAwf is with the Supreme Assembly among those whom God has favoured: the Prophets, the Veracious, the Martyrs, and the Virtuous; and the best of company are they. ʿAbd al-Malik and al-Ḥajjāj are dragging their guts in the Fire."[321] Imām Suyūṭī adds, "This was some time before ʿAbd al-Malik and Ḥajjāj took charge, for Miswar died in Makka on the same day when news was received of the death of Yazīd, the son of Muʿāwiya, in the year 64 AH, whereas Ḥajjāj did not assume office until after 70 AH.'"[322]

The Umayyad caliph ʿUmar ibn ʿAbd al-ʿAzīz asked to be sat up in bed during his last illness, and then he repeated thrice, "I am the one whom You commanded to do [good] but who fell short, whom You commanded not to commit [evil] but who did so, but for *Lā ilāha illa'llāh*!" He then raised his head and gazed intently, so those about him remarked, "How intently you gaze, O Commander of the Faithful!" He explained, "I see a presence that is neither human nor jinn," and then he died.[323] In Ibn Kathīr's version, recorded in his *Bidāya*, the caliph ordered everyone out. His relatives who then sat at his door heard him saying, "Welcome to those whose faces are neither human nor jinn." Then he recited: ***That is the Final Abode that We have made for those who desire no exaltation in the earth, nor corruption. The good end is for the God-fearing.***[324] Then all went quiet, so they entered and found that he had closed his eyes, turned himself toward the qibla and died.[325]

Fuḍāla ibn Dīnār reported that as he was attending Muḥammad ibn Wāsiʿ al-Azdī,[i] during his terminal illness, he heard him say, "Welcome

---

i Fuḍāla ibn Dīnār al-Shaḥḥām of Baṣra and Muḥammad ibn Wāsiʿ al-Azdī were both well-known scholars, traditionists and men of God of the third generation, that of the Followers of the Followers. They died in the second century of the Hijra.

to my Lord's angels, there is neither power nor ability save by God." Then Ibn Wāsiʿ smelled such a fragrant scent as he had never experienced before, and thereafter turned his gaze upward and died.[326]

Al-Ḥasan ibn Ṣāliḥ,[i] a Follower of the Followers, visited his brother ʿAlī on the day he died and asked him, "How are you?" He answered: ***With those whom God has favoured: the Prophets, the Veracious, the Martyrs and the Virtuous; and the best of company those are.***"[327] He thought he was just reciting the verse, so he repeated his question and received the same answer. So he asked him again, "Are you reciting or do you see something?" ʿAlī said, "Do you not see what I see?" He said, "No, what do you see?" He raised his hand and replied, "This is God's Prophet Muḥammad ﷺ smiling at me and giving the glad news of the Garden, and these are the angels with him, with silk and brocaded clothes in their hands, and those are the wide-eyed maidens in their full attire waiting for me to join them." No sooner had he finished his sentence than he died.[328]

Imām Suyūṭī reports that Imām Muḥammad al-Bāqir had said, "Every dying person sees the images of his good and evil deeds. He looks at his good deeds and turns his gaze away from his evil ones." He also reports that Ḥasan al-Baṣrī commented on the verse, ***Man shall be told on that day of what he has sent forward and what he has left behind***,[329] by saying, "The angels of death come down to him and both good and evil are shown to him; when what he sees is good he smiles, but when what he sees is evil he frowns and turns away.[330]

The Companion Yazīd ibn Shajara said that whenever a person is about to die he is shown images of his close friends, whether they are people given to frivolity or are people of remembrance.[331]

The Prophet ﷺ is reported to have said, "*When the Angel of Death comes to God's protégé he greets him with peace, and his greeting is that he says, 'May peace be upon you, O protégé of God. Rise and leave this abode that you have ruined for one that you have made prosperous.' If he is not one of God's protégés he shall say to him, 'Rise! Leave this abode that you have made prosperous for one you have ruined.'*"[332]

---

i Al-Ḥasan ibn Ṣāliḥ was a well-known scholar and transmitter of *ḥadīth* of the third generation. He died in 167 AH His brother ʿAlī was better known as an ascetic.

INTERACTIONS BETWEEN THE WORLD OF THE DEAD AND THE WORLD OF THE LIVING

ʿIkrima[i] was asked, "Does the blind person see the Angel of Death?" He answered, "Yes," a clear indication that this vision is one in which the eye of the heart beholds the World of Similitudes, not that of the physical eye.[333]

As *Sayyid* Muḥammad ibn ʿUmar Bā-ʿAlawī[ii] was dying, those around him heard a voice reciting: ***Their Lord gives them glad tidings of mercy from Him and immense satisfaction, and gardens wherein they shall have lasting bliss, perpetually immortal therein. God has an immense recompense.***[334] When he expired, the place was filled with such a light that it eclipsed the light of the lamp.[335]

---

i ʿIkrima, a Follower, was a disciple of Ibn ʿAbbās who taught him the religious sciences, especially Qurʾānic exegesis. He died in 104 or 107 AH.

ii *Sayyid* Muḥammad ibn ʿUmar Bā-ʿAlawī, known as *Sāhib al-Masaff*, was a well known scholar and saint who died in 822 AH.

10
Happenings in the Grave

When the Prophet ﷺ speaks of the grave, he does not mean the sandy pit where the bodies of the dead are buried, but the Intermediary World, where their spirits survive. This world is termed intermediary because it separates life in this world from life after resurrection. Among what he told his Companions was that once a man is buried and those who have escorted him start walking away he clearly hears their footsteps. Then two great angels arrive, sit him up, and interrogate him about his creed and about the Prophet ﷺ. Should his answer be that he is the Messenger of God ﷺ, they shall let him see his place in Paradise.[336] These two angels are black and terrifying. One is called Munkar and the other is Nakīr. Their task is to interrogate every dead person about his beliefs. Should he answer appropriately, his grave expands to seventy cubits, and is then filled with light.[337]

The Prophet ﷺ said, "*When the servant is placed in his grave and the people walk away, he hears the sounds of their sandals. Then the two angels arrive, sit him up, and ask him, 'What have you been saying about this man, Muḥammad?' If he says, 'I bear witness that he is the servant of God and His Messenger,' he is told, 'Look at your seat in the Fire, for it has been replaced with a place in the Garden.' Then he is given to see both. As for the disbeliever or the hypocrite, he will say, 'I do not know: I repeated what I heard other people say.' He will then be shown his seat in the Fire.*"[338] In this *ḥadīth*, we have a description of the happenings in the subtle dimension that follow death in this world. This is obviously a dimension different from the material one, for were one to open the grave, one would see nothing but the body that has just been buried, and not the dead man sitting up, being questioned by the angels, nor the place in Paradise or Hell that he is being shown, as the case may be. Also, the question of the angels, "What have you been saying about this man, Muḥammad?" indicates that the dead man is given to see the Prophet ﷺ

or "this man", so as to be able to identify him.

He also explained to them that the grave is either a meadow of Paradise or a pit in the Fire. In addition, he informed them that the grave speaks to the believer and greets and welcomes him as soon as he is buried, then expands as far as his vision reaches and opens a door onto Paradise for him.[339] And he ﷺ said that in the grave people are shown their place in the Garden or the Fire according to their states.[340]

When the dead person is a believer, his ritual prayers come from his head, his *zakāt* from his right side, his fasts from his left side, and the good he has done to others and his benevolent deeds from his feet. When the believer's head is threatened his ritual prayer will say, "He cannot be got at from my side." When threatened from his right side his *zakāt* will say, "He cannot be got at from my side." When threatened from his left side his fasts will say, "He cannot be got at from my side." When his feet are threatened his good deeds and his benevolence will say, "He cannot be got at from our side." Then they will sit him up and question him; and when he answers that he knows that the Prophet ﷺ is indeed the Messenger of God whom he has believed and followed, he is told, "You have spoken the truth, according to that you have lived and died and according to that you will be resurrected, God willing, secure." Then his grave is enlarged for as far as his eyes can see, and then it will be said, "Open a door for him to the Fire." When it is done he is told, "This would have been your dwelling had you disobeyed God." At which his joy and happiness increase. Then it will be said, "Open a door for him onto the Garden," and when it is opened he is told, "This is your dwelling: what God has prepared for you," and he becomes more joyful and happy. Then his body is returned to its origin in the dust, while his spirit remains in Heaven.[341]

Abū Hurayra and Ibn Masʿūd both reported that the Prophet ﷺ had told them to bury their dead among virtuous people, for the dead are offended by evil neighbours just as the living are.[342]

It seems that the Lady Sawda, the Prophet's wife, understood well that after they die virtuous people are still able to benefit others, for she once asked the Prophet, "O Messenger of God, once we die, ʿUthmān ibn Maẓʿūn will pray for us until you come to us?" He answered, "*Had you the knowledge of death, O daughter of Zamʿa, you would have known that it is harder than you imagine.*"[343] ʿUthmān ibn Maẓʿūn had been the first Companion to be buried in the Baqīʿ Cemetery and Lady Sawda expected him to pray for them once they died and rejoined him, an expectation that the Prophet ﷺ tacitly approved, for in his answer to her he merely pointed out that before they rejoined him they would have to undergo death itself and should be more concerned about that. It stands to reason that if the dead are capable of praying for their fellow dead, they would also be capable of praying for the living and thus benefitting them with their prayers.

Abū Saʿid al-Khudrī recounted how he accompanied the Prophet ﷺ to the funeral of Saʿd ibn Muʿādh. When they were digging his grave a fragrance of musk emanated from the dirt.[344] The Companions asked the Prophet ﷺ why he was in such a hurry to convey Saʿd to his grave in Baqīʿ Cemetery and he told them he was anxious lest the angels precede them as they had done with Ḥanẓala whom they had washed on the battlefield of Uḥud. They remarked on how Saʿd was a heavy man, yet they had never carried a lighter bier, which the Prophet ﷺ explained by saying that he had seen the angels carrying him.[345]

The burial of Saʿd ibn Muʿādh seems to be the first time when another of the happenings of the grave was mentioned by the Prophet ﷺ. That was the squeezing that each dead person undergoes immediately after death, before being questioned by the two angels. ʿĀ'isha later said that the Prophet ﷺ had said that there is a squeezing in the grave and that were anyone to escape it, it would have been Saʿd ibn Muʿādh.[346] Jābir said, "When we buried Saʿd ibn Muʿādh, the Messenger of God ﷺ raised his voice with *tasbīḥ*, and we repeated the *tasbīḥ* with him for a while, then he raised it with *takbīr*[i], and we repeated the *takbīr* with him. Then the people asked, "O Messenger of God, why did you do *tasbīḥ*?" He answered, "*The grave of this good man had tightened around him, and then God relieved him through His mercy.*"[347] This means that the Prophet ﷺ saw that his Companion was being squeezed in the Intermediary World and sought to assist him through the invocation of *tasbīḥ*, then he saw him being released and responded with the joyous exclamation of *takbīr*.

---

i *Takbīr* is to glorify God by saying, "*Allāh akbar*" (God is the greatest).

Ḥudhayfa said that he had once attended a funeral with the Prophet ﷺ and when they had reached the edge of the grave, he looked at it intently, then said, "*The believer is squeezed in it with such force that his chest is crushed; as for the disbeliever, it is filled with fire around him.*" Then he continued, "*Shall I tell you who the worst of God's servants are? They are those who are coarse and arrogant. Shall I tell you who the best of God's servants are? They are those who are weak and humble, wrapped in two ragged cloths, yet when they beseech God, He responds to their satisfaction.*"[348]

Yaʿlā ibn Murra said, "We passed by some graves in the company of the Messenger of God ﷺ and I heard a squeezing in one of them. I said, 'O Messenger of God, I heard a squeezing in one of these graves.' He asked, '*Did you hear it, Yaʿlā?*' and I answered, 'Yes.' So he said, '*He is being punished for something that is not so serious.*' I asked, 'May God ransom me for you, what is it?' He said, '*He was a seditious man who spread gossip among the people and he did not purify himself thoroughly from urine.*'"[349]

Ibn ʿAbbās related how when ʿAlī's mother Fāṭima bint Asad died, the Prophet ﷺ removed his tunic, dressed her in it, then lay down in her grave prior to burying her. When they asked him about it, remarking that he had done something they had never seen him do before, he said that he had clothed her in his tunic so that she would be clothed in the raiment of Paradise and that he had laid down in her grave to lighten the squeezing on her, for after Abū Ṭālib she had been the created being who had done him the most good.[350]

One day the Prophet ﷺ inquired after a black woman who used to clean the mosque and was told she had died. He asked them why they had not informed him and was made to understand that she was really of no consequence. He asked them to take him to her grave and there he performed her funeral prayer. He then said, "*These graves are filled with shadows upon their occupants and God illuminates them by my prayers on them.*"[351]

The famous Follower Thābit al-Bunānī, the beloved student of the Companion and servant of the Prophet ﷺ Anas ibn Mālik, was often heard praying, "O God, if You have ever granted anyone to pray in his grave, then grant it to me!"[352] After his death one of his friends swore that he had seen him in a dream-vision wearing green clothes standing in prayer in his grave.[353] Then it was recounted by many who passed by his grave in the early hours of the morning that they heard the sound of Qur'ān recitation coming from it.[354]

Sufyān ibn 'Uyayna's cousin said, "When my father died I was deeply aggrieved and took to visiting him every day, but then I eventually stopped. After a while, I returned and whilst near the grave I was overcome by sleep and saw my father sitting in his grave, wrapped in his shroud, pale with a deathly pallor. He said, "My son, what kept you away?" I asked in turn, "Are you aware of my visit every time I come?" He answered, "Not once did you come without my knowing it and when you used to come your prayers gladdened me and the people around me."

The Prophet ﷺ said, "*The believer's grave is in a green meadow. It is enlarged for him by seventy cubits, and its light is like the full moon's.*"[355]

'Abd al-Raḥmān ibn 'Umāra ibn 'Uqba ibn Abī Mu'ayṭ[i] said that he attended the funeral of al-Aḥnaf ibn Qays[ii] in Kufa and was one of those who went down into the grave to receive him. He reported that once they had laid him down, he saw the grave expand as far as the eye could see. When he told those who were with him, none of them had seen what he had just witnessed.[356]

The Prophet ﷺ said that when a learned man dies, his knowledge is given a form in his grave to comfort him until the Day of Resurrection and keep away the creatures of the earth.[357]

God revealed to Moses, "Learn what is good and teach it to the people, for I shall illuminate the graves of both the teacher [and his student] so that they never feel estranged."[358]

The Prophet ﷺ has informed us that the dead are affected by other

---

i 'Uqba ibn Abī Mu'ayṭ was an arch enemy of the Prophet ﷺ who ferociously opposed his mission in Makka. He was taken captive during the Battle of Badr and executed on the way back. His son, 'Umāra ibn 'Uqba, accepted Islām after the Conquest of Makka, thus becoming a Companion of the Prophet ﷺ. 'Abd al-Raḥmān ibn 'Umāra, 'Uqba's grandson was a Follower, a disciple of the Companions. Their dates of death are unrecorded.

ii Companion of the Prophet ﷺ who fought on the side of Imām 'Alī in Siffīn and died in 67 or 71 AH.

deceased people around them. He ﷺ said, "*Bury your dead in the midst of virtuous people, for the dead are as offended as the living by evil neighbours.*"[359] He ﷺ also said, "*When one of your kin dies shroud him well, execute his will swiftly, deepen his grave, and avoid evil neighbours.*" He was asked, "O Messenger of God, would a good neighbour be of any benefit in the Hereafter?" He replied, "*Is he of benefit in this world?*" They answered affirmatively and he said, "*So will he be of benefit in the Hereafter.*"[360]

A man from Madina once saw in a dream-vision that an acquaintance of his who had just died was in the Fire, which distressed him greatly. Seven or eight nights later he saw him again, but this time he was in the Garden. He asked him about it and was told, "A man of God was buried among us and has been permitted to intercede for forty of his neighbours, and I was among them."[361]

11

The Experience of God

THE VOICE OF GOD

God spoke to Adam in the Garden of Eden,[362] and then again after he came down to earth.[363] Thereafter, God spoke to his Prophets: ***It belongs not to any human being that God should speak to him, except by revelation, from behind a veil, or that He should send an Envoy who will reveal whatsoever He will by His leave.***[364] Revelation here means what God casts directly into the hearts of His Envoys, while from behind a veil means that they hear the voice, but see nothing. Here scholars are very careful to stress that God the Absolute cannot be veiled, but it is the servant who is veiled out of compassion for him, for otherwise he would not be able to withstand meeting his Lord unveiled. The third mode is for the Angel of Revelation, Gabriel, to descend upon the Envoy, either in his heart or outwardly in human form, to deliver the Divine message.

As the Qur'ān tells us, God spoke to Moses many times: first from the burning bush,[365] then face-to-face on Mount Sinai.[366] Now Divine speech originates in the eternal knowledge of God and cannot be contained by time, space, form or any other limits. Thus, for a human being, however tremendous his spiritual rank, to hear the speech of God, that speech must have reached him in a form suitable for the conditions of this world. The many degrees of descent of that speech to reach Moses in an appropriate mode will have necessarily taken place in the World of Similitudes. The burning bush itself is a manifestation of that world.

Divine speech was also heard by the Prophet ﷺ at the pinnacle of his Ascension, beyond the seven heavens and the Divine Throne.

The Prophet ﷺ said to Jābir ibn ʿAbdallāh concerning his father who had been martyred at Uḥud, "*God never spoke to anyone save from be-*

hind a veil. However, He brought your father back to life and spoke to him face-to-face. He asked him, 'My servant, wish for anything from Me and I shall grant it to you!' He said, 'Lord, revive me so that I may be slain for Your sake again!' He said, 'It has already been decreed that they shall never return to it.'"[367] The first statement, namely that God never speaks to anyone save from behind a veil, concerns this world. The next statement, that He spoke to him face-to-face, concerns the *Barzakh* where the lofty state of the martyrs becomes manifest.

The following *ḥadīth* concerns the Hereafter: "*Each one of you will be spoken to by His Lord with no mediator between them or a veil that veils him.*"[368]

Ibn ʿAbbās said that when Adam was sent down to earth he said to God, "O Lord, why can I not hear the voices of the angels, nor feel their presence?" He answered, "Your sin, O Adam; but go and build Me a house, circle around it, remember Me there, just as you have seen the angels do around My Throne."[369]

The Garden and the Fire are capable of speaking in their world, both to each other and to God. The Prophet ﷺ stated that the Garden and the Fire once argued before God. The Garden asking why it was that only the meekest entered it, and the Fire why only the most arrogant entered it. God spoke to the Garden saying that it was His mercy and to the Fire saying it was His wrath and that each would receive its fill in due course.[370] He ﷺ also said that the Fire once complained to God that it was consuming itself.[371]

THE VISION OF GOD

The Qur'ān states explicitly that God will be seen in the Hereafter: ***That day some faces will be radiant, gazing upon their Lord***.[372] And the Prophet ﷺ confirmed this many times: one of them on a night when the moon was full and he said, "*You shall see your Lord just as you see this moon and you shall suffer no difficulty in seeing Him.*"[373]

The people asked the Prophet ﷺ, "Shall we see our Lord on Resurrection Day?" He answered, "*Do you experience any difficulty in seeing the moon on the night when it is full?*" They said, "No, O Messenger of God." He asked, "*Do you experience any difficulty in seeing the sun when there are no clouds?"* They said, "No, O Messenger of God." He said, "*Thus will you see Him. God will gather the people on the Day of Resurrection and say, 'Those who worshipped anything let them follow it. Those who used to worship the sun will follow the sun and those who used to worship the moon will follow the moon, and those who used to worship idols will follow those idols. There shall be left this community with its intercessors.' God shall come to them, saying, 'I am your Lord.' [Not recognising Him] they will say, 'We will stay here until our Lord comes. When He comes we will recognise him.' Then God shall come in the very form they know and shall say, 'I am your Lord.' They will answer, 'Indeed, you are our Lord,' and they will follow Him. The Bridge will be erected over Hell and I and my community shall be the first to cross.*"[374] The *ḥadīth* is a long one. It describes at length the events of the Day of Resurrection, before going on to describe a long conversation between God and a man, initially destined for the Fire, but who will eventually enter the Garden and be the very last to do so.

In explanation of the verse that says, ***For those who have done well there shall be a reward most fair and a surplus***,[375] the Prophet ﷺ said, "*Once the people of the Garden have entered it, a herald will cry, 'You have a meeting with God.' They will ask, 'Has He not made our faces white, saved us from the Fire and admitted us to the Garden?' They will be answered, 'Yes.' Then the veil shall be removed and, by God, nothing that has been given to them will be dearer to them than gazing at Him.*"[376]

12
Unveiling

IMĀM GHAZĀLĪ ON UNVEILING

Discussing the phenomenon of unveiling, Imām Ghazālī says in his *Iḥyā'*:

If you say, "How does the Devil take the form of some people but not others? And when a form is seen, is this his true form or just an image? And if it is his true form, how can he also be seen in other different forms? And how can he be seen in two different places and in two different forms at the same time, so that two persons will see two different forms?" Know that an angel and a devil both have forms that are their real ones and these can only be seen by the light of prophethood. The Prophet ﷺ saw Gabriel in his true form only twice, but usually saw him in the form of Diḥya al-Kalbī.

The people of unveiling see the Devil while awake. They see him with their physical eyes and hear his voice with their physical ears. The people of unveiling are those who have reached a stage where the engagement of their senses with material worldly things does not prevent them from seeing in their waking states what others only see in their dreams.

It has been reported that 'Umar ibn 'Abd al-'Azīz said that a man had asked his Lord to show him where the Devil is situated within the heart of human beings. He saw in his dream a human body made of something like glass, so that its inside could be seen externally. He then saw the Devil in the form of a toad, sitting on his left shoulder, between his shoulder and his ear. It had a long thin trunk that penetrated through the left shoulder into the heart to whisper things to him. When the man remembered God, it retreated. Such a vision may be seen while awake as well. Another man of unveiling saw the Devil in the form of a dog crouching on a carcass (or this world) inviting people to [partake of] it.

The heart must necessarily manifest a reality from its aspect that faces the Invisible World (*Malakūt*), then the effects will dawn on its aspect facing the Visible World (*Mulk*), for the two are connected. We have already explained that the heart has two aspects: one turned toward the Invisible World and constituting an entrance for inspiration and revelation, and the other turned toward the Visible World. The aspect turned toward the Visible World perceives the images grasped by the physical senses and projected onto the mind with the faculty of its imagination. However, this image may or may not be consonant with the inward reality of the being that is perceived. A good-looking person, for instance, may be inwardly evil, in which case the inner reality is belied by the appearance. On the other hand, the image that is reflected in the imagination from the Invisible World through the illuminated inner aspect of the heart always conforms to the inner reality. Thus, when the Devil appears in the form of a toad or a dog, this form is sufficiently repulsive to conform to the inner reality it represents. Evil realities appear in the forms of monkeys and pigs, while a virtuous man may be represented by a sheep for instance, as in dreams.[377]

DIMENSIONS OF UNVEILING

Unveiling, however, may take many forms that seem qualitatively different from witnessing the World of Similitudes, although there is frequent overlapping between the two. These consist in the capacity of one's powers of spiritual perception to penetrate the veils that ordinarily prevent us from seeing or hearing events that are at a distance, or hidden by a material barrier, or perceive the thoughts and feelings inside someone's head.

An example of perception at a distance is the Prophet ﷺ seeing his Companions fighting a desperate battle far away in the north of the Arabian peninsula. Tears streaming down his face, he recounted what he was seeing to those around him in Madina. He said that Zayd had held the banner until he was killed, then it was taken by Jaʿfar who guarded it until he was slain, then it was taken by ʿAbdallāh ibn Rawāḥa who raised it until he was slaughtered, then Khālid ibn al-Walīd took it without having been commissioned and victory was granted to him.[378]

Another example occurred the day he informed the Companions that the Negus of Abyssinia, who had given asylum to some Companions who migrated there from Makka, had died. He then took them out to the *Muṣallā*, the open space to the west of the city, where they performed the funeral prayer.[379]

Yet another instance occurred after the battle of Badr, when ʿUmayr ibn Wahb came from Makka to Madina, ostensibly to ransom a relative of his who had been taken captive, but in reality intending to assassinate the Prophet ﷺ. ʿUmar, sitting in a group of Companions, saw him put his camel to rest and enter the mosque. Worried about his intentions, he gripped him tightly by the collar and dragged him before the Prophet ﷺ, who said, "*Let go of him, ʿUmar. Come nearer to me ʿUmayr!*" When he did so, the Prophet ﷺ asked him what had brought him to Madina, and he answered that he wished to ransom his captured relative. The Prophet ﷺ said, "*Not so, for you sat with Ṣafwān ibn Umayya in the Ḥijr and agreed that he would look after your family exactly as he looks after his own, on the precondition that you would ride here and kill me.*" ʿUmayr was astounded; he swore to the Prophet ﷺ that there had been none in the Ḥijr but the two of them and that only God could have informed him. Then he uttered the two testimonies, thus declaring his Islām, following which the Prophet ﷺ said to his Companions, "*Instruct your brother in his religion, teach him the Qurʾān and release his prisoner to him.*"[380] Here we see how the Prophet ﷺ, through his powers of unveiling, actually saw and heard what had been happening three hundred miles away in Makka.

As for reading thoughts, even at a distance, the following incident is a good example. When Qubāth ibn Ashyam al-Kinānī came to Madina to find out how things were developing, he sought the Prophet ﷺ among a group of his Companions and could not identify him. The Prophet ﷺ addressed him first, saying, "*O Qubāth ibn Ashyam, are you the one who said on the Day of Badr, 'I have never seen anyone flee such a situation but women.*'" Hearing this, he exclaimed, "I bear witness that you are the Messenger of God! This was heard by no one at all; they were but words I whispered to myself. Had you not been a Prophet, God would not have revealed them to you. I shall now pledge my allegiance to you."[381]

The Companions also had powers of unveiling. 'Ā'isha said that in his last moments her father Abū Bakr sat up, uttered the *shahāda*, then told her that she should share what he was bequeathing them with her two brothers and two sisters. She asked him what he meant by two sisters, since she had only a sister, Asmā'. He replied that one of his wives, Khārija's daughter, was pregnant with a girl.[382] Abū Bakr had seen that the child in his wife's womb was a girl.

The third caliph, 'Uthmān ibn 'Affān, is also reported to have possessed the power of unveiling. Once a man came to visit him who had just looked at a woman on the street. He said, "Does one of you come to me with the trace of adultery clearly to be seen in his eyes?" The visitor said, "What, revelation after the Messenger of God?" He replied, "No, but insight, proof and true perspicacity."[383]

Nāfi' al-Qāri' was a master of Qur'ān recitation of the second century of the Hijra. Whenever he spoke the scent of musk came out of his mouth. He was asked, "Do you perfume yourself every time you sit?" He replied, "I never touch perfume, but I saw the Prophet ﷺ in my dream reciting into my mouth. Since then this scent comes out of me."[384]

Abu'l-Ḥasan al-Būshinjī and al-Ḥasan al-Ḥaddād, both Sufi masters of the fourth century of the Hijra, once visited another master, Abu'l-Qāsim al-Munāwī. On their way they had bought a single apple worth half a dirham but omitted to pay for it, each thinking that the other had done so, leaving the vendor too embarrassed to ask for his money. As soon as he saw them, Munāwī exclaimed, "What is all this darkness?" They retreated and once outside the house said to each other, "What might this be? Perhaps it is the apple?" Having discovered that they had not paid for it, they retraced their steps to the vendor, handed him the price of the apple, and then returned to the Shaykh. As soon as he set eyes on them he said, "Can someone get rid of his darkness this quickly? Tell me what you have done," so they told him.[385]

Ibrāhīm al-Khawwāṣ said, "I was in the mosque when a handsome young man, dignified and smelling perfumed, entered. I said to my companions, 'I think he is Jewish.' They were all annoyed by this. Both I and the young man left the mosque, but he returned and asked them, 'What did the Shaykh say about me?' They were reluctant to tell him, but he insisted so much that they told him the Shaykh had said he was a Jew. He came after me, kissed my hand and became a Muslim. I asked him why he had done so and he answered, 'We find in our Book that the perspicacity of a *Ṣiddīq* is never wrong. I said to myself, "I shall test the Muslims. I observed them and concluded that if there was a *Ṣiddīq* among them he would be from this sect [meaning the Sufis]." So I tried to deceive you, but when you found me out, I knew you were a *Ṣiddīq*.'"[386]

When the people of the town of Ḥarrān in Syria built a mosque they invited the famous Shaykh Ḥayāt ibn Qays al-Ḥarrānī[i] to attend to help orient the *miḥrāb*. The architect said, "The qibla is in this direction." The Shaykh disagreed and to prove himself right said to him, "Look, and you shall see the Kaʿba!" Suddenly, the architect found himself looking straight at it, seeing it clearly. He fainted.[387]

Shaykh Abu'l–Ḥasan al-Shādhilī said when his heart was illuminated one day and he was witnessing the dominion of the seven heavens and the seven earths, he committed a triviality and was immediately veiled from his vision. He was surprised at how such a small matter veiled him from such a mighty matter, and he heard a voice saying to him, "The inner sight is like the eyesight: the least of things that get in it obstruct its vision."[388]

The scholar and traditionist *Sayyid* ʿAbd al-Raḥmān ibn al-Shaykh ʿAlī al-Saqqāf who died in 923 AH was a man whose powers of unveiling were often noticed by his companions. Among them was another great scholar, *Sayyid* Muḥammad ibn ʿAlī Khirid. He said, "I saw the Lord of Might in a dream describing our shaykh in a complimentary manner. As soon as I woke up in the morning I went to him, saying to myself, 'If he is a man of unveiling, he will inform me of it before I tell

---

i Shaykh Ḥayāt ibn Qays al-Ḥarrānī was a great scholar and famous saint of Harran in Northern Iraq who was sometimes consulted by Saladin (Salāh al-Dīn al-Ayyūbī) about his strategy. He died in 581 AH.

him.' When I reached his house I found him standing outside, waiting for me. He then told me about all I had seen before I had time to tell him."[389]

Walking down the street on his way to the *zāwiya* for prayer, the imām of Shaykh Muḥammad ibn ʿAnān's *zāwiya* noticed a pretty woman and gazed at her. He entered the *zāwiya* only to find the Shaykh bidding someone else to lead the prayer. The time for the next prayer came and the Shaykh did the same, and then repeatedly until five prayers had been completed. It finally dawned on him that the Shaykh had seen that gaze, at which point he immediately asked God for forgiveness.[390]

When Shaykh al-Islām Ibn Ḥajar passed by Shaykh Muḥammad al-Farghal one day, he thought to himself how unlikely it was that God should make such an ignorant man a saint of His, for were He to make him a saint, He would have taught him. Immediately, the Shaykh cried, "Halt, O judge!" He then grabbed him and proceeded to beat and slap him across the face, crying, "He has in fact made me [a saint] and He has in fact taught me!"[391]

There was a woman in a faraway country who believed strongly in Shaykh Muḥammad al-Farghal's sanctity. She had a sick son and one day vowed that if God were to cure her son, she would make a carpet for the Shaykh. God granted what she desired and she proceeded to fulfil her vow. In his hometown in Upper Egypt, the Shaykh was heard saying, "They are now spinning the wool for the carpet." Then periodically he would say, "They are now winding the wool on the yarn"; "They are now beginning to weave it"; "They have sent it"; "They are now unloading it off the ship"; and "They have now arrived at such-and-such a spot." Until one day he finally said, "Let someone go out and receive the carpet, for it has arrived at the door." They went and found the men standing at the door waiting to deliver it, just as the Shaykh had told them.[392]

Shaykh ʿUthmān al-Khaṭṭāb began building a mosque in Cairo. Part of the land was occupied by a brothel. He went up to the citadel and said to the Sultan that this piece of land used to be a mosque, but had been demolished and built over as it now was; so according to the Sacred Law, when a mosque is demolished a new one has to be rebuilt in its place. Since the Sultan believed the Shaykh to be entirely trustworthy, he accepted his assertion and ordered the new building to be demolished and handed over to the Shaykh to complete his *zāwiya*. Yet the owners of the building bribed a judge to go to the Sultan and tell him that he should not risk embarrassment by demolishing a building solely on the authority of a mad Sufi. The Sultan, however, replied that he believed what the Shaykh had told him. When the building was demolished as ordered, the *miḥrāb* of the old mosque appeared and its two flanking pillars. The Shaykh then sent word to the Sultan who came down to see for himself.[393]

As a disciple was once sitting facing Shaykh ʿAbd al-ʿAzīz al-Dabbāgh, who was leaning half asleep on a cushion, an evil thought crossed his mind. The Shaykh immediately opened his eyes and asked, "What did you say?" He replied, "Sīdī, I said nothing." The Shaykh retorted, "What did you say in your heart?"

The same Shaykh is reported to have said that on Thursday, 8th Rajab 1125 AH, he had left his house for the market. Somewhere along the way he began to shiver, then tremble all over, then feel numb. His breathing became extremely uneven and he felt he was about to die. He said, "Then something like vapour came out of my body and gradually things became unveiled before me. I began to see the towns, villages and everything across the land, then the seas, the seven earths and all the creatures they contain. I saw the sky as if I had been raised high above it, looking down at what it contains. A tremendous light, a flashing lightning, came from every direction at once, making me very cold. I thought I had died. I threw myself down on the ground, covering my face so as not to see that light, but I found that every part of me was able to see. My clothes were preventing no part of me from seeing." He remained in that state for a while, before returning to his normal frame of mind. He felt greatly disturbed, was tearful, and felt incapable of carrying on to the market, and so returned home. The same state overcame him over and over again, each time lingering with him a while longer. Eventually he became accustomed to it and it became his permanent state.

The Shaykh once remarked, "People are fond of unveilings, but they carry great risks, both for the saint and for those who desire them. The first is because he has to come down from witnessing the Real to witnessing creation, an obvious fall from the highest summit; and the second is because seekers of unveilings and supernatural events are shaky in their love for the saint and should he give them what they seek, he would be confirming them in their condition and helping to keep them there."

The eye of the heart is the organ that perceives the Divine Names and Attributes and to use it to look at the physical or even the subtle worlds is to misuse it. Once open, the saint is capable of seeing higher and higher levels of existence, but also of penetrating through dense bodies across time and space. Speaking of the inner eye, the Shaykh said, "When directed at any particular thing it penetrates all obstacles. Once the image of that thing becomes clear to the Eye of the Heart and the latter has reached the degree of perfection, it includes the [physical] eyesight and that image will be seen by the eyes, but superimposed on whatever is in front of them, whether it be a wall, a paper or his hand. Thus it was that when the Prophet ﷺ directed his eye of the heart toward Paradise and Hell, he beheld them on the wall before him."

Contrary to the vast majority of similarly qualified people, the Shaykh's particular relationship with his Lord permitted him to reveal how he was able to do such things. Thus it was that he once explained that Prophetic utterances were accompanied with light, while ordinary ones were not. Furthermore, when they heard these utterances, Knowers by God[i] felt their own lights grow brighter, but not so with ordinary speech. On another occasion when Ibn al-Mubārak kept quoting to him verses from the Qur'ān and sayings of the Prophet ﷺ, the Shaykh unerringly distinguished between each of them, following which he explained that, although they had all come from the Prophet ﷺ and had lights of his lights, the light of the Qur'ān was pre-existent, from the Essence of the Real, for His words are pre-existent; and the light of the *Ḥadīth Qudsī* came from the Prophet's spirit and that of the *Ḥadīth Nabawī* from the Prophet's body. The body being made of dust is attracted to the rest of creation, while the spirit is from the Sublime Assembly and they are those who, out of all creation, have the most

i Knower by God ('Ārif b'illāh) is the saint who sees, hears, and moves by God, according to the Ḥadīth Qudsi that states that once God loves one of His servants He becomes the eye with which he sees, the ear with which he hears.

direct knowledge of the Real. Each yearns for its origin. The light of the spirit is attracted to the Real and that of the body to creation. Thus does the *Ḥadīth Qudsī* relate to the Real, His magnitude, mercy, generosity, and so on. The *Ḥadīth Nabawī*, on the other hand, relates to practical matters of what is licit and illicit, transactions between creatures, and other such things. The lights of the Real descend on the body of the Prophet ﷺ and, although he is perpetually in a state of witnessing, they result in special kinds of witnessing. When together with the lights that are alighting he also hears the words of the Real or the angels descend upon him: this is the Qur'ān. When he hears no words and no angel descends, he speaks of what he witnesses of God and that becomes *Ḥadīth Qudsī*. Finally, what he speaks of in an ordinary state of witnessing comes out with the light of his body and becomes *Ḥadīth Nabawī*. The words of the Prophet ﷺ are always accompanied by the lights of God, but different kinds of light accompany different kinds of speech. When the Prophet ﷺ is compelled to speak, that is the Qur'ān. When he speaks out of choice, the utterance is a *ḥadīth*. At that time, either exceptional lights are alighting upon him, and the result will be a *Ḥadīth Qudsī*, or the lights are only those that are permanently with him, in which case the result wll be a *Ḥadīth Nabawī*.

More recently, Shaykh Aḥmad Ḥijāb recounted how he and his brother were sitting with their spiritual master *Sayyid* Muḥammad al-Sharīf in Ṭanṭā, Egypt, and he asked them, "Does your father wear a red-felt cap under his turban?" They knew he had never seen him wear one. They answered, "He has never worn one." He said nothing for a short while, and then said, "Both of you go now to meet your father at the station." They said, "The Manṣūra train does not reach Ṭanṭā until 1.20 in the afternoon." He repeated, "Both of you go now to meet him." They rose and headed for the station. Sure enough, their father arrived wearing a red-felt cap under his turban and proceeded to explain to them how he had modified his schedule to reach Ṭanṭā at that unusual hour.[394]

PERCEPTION OF THE INNER REALITY OF PEOPLE

Shaykh Muḥyiddīn ibn ʿArabī says in his *Futūḥāt* that among the men of God he had met in his travels who were able to see the subtle realities of people was one who saw the extremists among the Shī'a, the Rawāfiḍ, in the form of pigs. When someone went by him trying to hide such beliefs, he would see him as a pig and call him over and tell him, "Repent to God, for you are a Rāfiḍī Shī'a." When the man accepted his advice and recanted with sincerity he saw him as a human being; but when he declared that he had repented but inwardly continued to maintain the same beliefs, he saw him as a pig still and told him, "You lie when you say you have repented."

Many times such people, faced with his powers of unveiling, did in fact recant and abandon the Rāfiḍī creed. This happened once with two men who were thought to be Shāfiʿī in their beliefs and just in their behaviour. They did not originate from a Shīʿī household, but had reached this position after some personal consideration. They began to think ill of Abū Bakr and ʿUmar and hold extreme views about ʿAlī, but decided to keep up appearances as Shāfiʿīs. When they came to the Shaykh he ordered them to be expelled, for God had revealed their inward state to him in the form of pigs, which was the sign He gave him by which to recognise the Rawāfiḍ. They objected – certain that none were aware of their beliefs but themselves – and assured all that they were well known as just Sunnī men, to which he answered that he saw them as pigs and that this was the sign God had given him for people like them. As both thought inwardly that they should repent, he told them, "You have renounced this creed at this moment, for I now see you as human," which impressed them even more and confirmed them in their repentance.[395]

Imām Shaʿrānī writes in his *al-Ṭabaqāt al-Kubrā* that it was reported to him that Shaykh Muḥammad al-Ḥanafī had said that he had stayed in his retreat for seven years and when he came out he saw a number of men performing their ritual ablutions at the fountain. He saw that some of them had faces like monkeys, others like pigs, and others like the moon. He realised that God was revealing to him the inner states of these people, so he stepped back and ardently implored Him to save him from this vision. He goes on to say that God responded by veiling the inner states of the people from him and he became like everyone else.[396]

In his *al-Ṭabaqāt al-Ṣughrā*, Imām Shaʿrānī writes that whenever he saw Shaykh Amīn al-Dīn ʿAbd al-ʿĀl, who died in 971 AH, he felt radiating from him an immense affection and comfort that filled all his senses; and he saw that his inward self was entirely free of the convolutions of the soul, as if it were that of a child. He adds that he felt nothing of the sort with any of the Shaykh's peers.[397] In the same book, he recounts that when Imām Shihāb al-Dīn al-Ramlī and his son Muḥammad came to visit him during an illness that almost led to his death, and the Shaykh was praying to God while his son was saying, "*Amīn!*" the prayers of the Shaykh were unveiled to him and he saw that they were uttered with such determination and power that they ascended to heaven like lightning.[398]

Imām Shaʿrānī also says that one night he saw unveiled before him the realities of the works of the scholars of al-Azhar. He saw them ascending to Heaven and he saw that the brightest were those of Shaykh Shams al-Dīn al-Barhamtūshī.[i] His immediate thought was that it was due to his utter sincerity.[399]

i He was an Egyptian Ḥanafī scholar, who died in 972 AH.

Conclusion

It should now be clear that there exists a multitude of dimensions that are hidden to our physical senses; and of these, some are Divine, which means uncreated, eternal and infinite, while others are created and so ephemeral and finite. The uncreated dimensions pertain to the Divine Essence and attributes, while the created dimensions include the heavenly spheres, the Throne, the Pedestal, Paradise, Hell, and the world of the jinn, as well as what pertains to the human being's body and soul. The physical world is perceived through the five senses, while everything else is hidden from our sense of perception. At times, some of the realities of the hidden world appear in the physical world and are then perceived by the senses. These manifestations of the hidden dimensions are termed the World of Similitudes. The images that appear in either the World of Dreams or the World of Similitudes are the forms assumed by intelligible realities to become perceptible, for intelligible realities, being formless, are beyond perception, whether by the physical senses or the imagination, and can only be apprehended by the intellect.

To recapitulate the essentials of the manifestations of the World of Similitudes that we have discussed, let us recall that the angels, among whom is the Angel of Death, appear either as subtle forms to be seen only by those possessed of a certain degree of unveiling, or in solid human form. They may also appear as birds or a wind and may be heard as disembodied voices. At the opposite end of the spectrum, Satan and his host of demons may appear either in subtle form, again to be seen only by people of unveiling, or in human, animal or reptile form. They can also be heard as voices.

The spirits of departed people can be seen in a subtle form, as well as in solid human form.

We know that life in the Intermediary World is a full life where the spirits take on subtle forms appropriate to that world. The more enlightened a spirit is, the freer it is to roam the worlds in all their dimensions; and the darker it is the more subject it is to severe conditions and restrictions. The Intermediary World is for some spirits a meadow of Paradise, full of blessings and lights, while for others it is a pit of Hell, full of horrors and shadows. The spirits of the believers are aware of much of what the living are doing. They are also aware of their visitors, hear them when they speak to them and answer, but in such a manner that most of the time only spiritual people can hear them.

Material things may appear from the Unseen. Examples of this are summer fruits appearing in the winter, or winter fruits in the summer, a white ram appearing to Abraham in Minā, a bucket of sweet cold water in the hot desert to Umm Ayman and Umm Sharīk, and a trench ablaze with fire to the obdurate pagan Abū Jahl. Fever appears to the Prophet ﷺ in the form of a dishevelled black woman who is not only seen but capable of conversing with him. This world appears in the form of a toothless white-haired old woman; the act of backbiting appears in the form of bloody flesh; and knowledge appears in the form of milk.

When the Prophet ﷺ is born his mother sees a light shine so powerfully that it illuminates the palaces of Syria, while those around her see it illuminating only the room they are in. On pitch black nights the tips of the staffs of the Companions shine with light until they reach home.

Things that are remote in time or space may be witnessed, for example the seditions that were to befall the people in Madina and which the Prophet ﷺ saw long before they happened as he stood on the rooftop of one of the city's bastions. On another occasion, the mosque in Jerusalem appeared nearer to him than the house of his cousin ʿAqīl in Makka, so that he was able to describe it to the pagans after his Night Journey. Events and realities of the Hereafter can also be seen in this world. The Prophet ﷺ described how death would be brought to the place separating Paradise from Hell, where it will be slaughtered while the denizens of both abodes are watching; how the Qur'ān and fasting will assume forms to intercede on behalf of those believers who did their due towards them; how *Sūra al-Baqara* and *Sūra Āl-ʿImrān* will come as two immense clouds to speak on behalf of those who recited them; and how the Black Stone and Yemeni Corner of the Kaʿba will have eyes, lips and tongues to testify on behalf of those who touched them with faith in this world.

Among the manifestations of the World of Similitudes are the Vision of God in the Hereafter and hearing His voice in both worlds. Other manifestations include that which dying people witness and the subtle forms taken by invocations, prayers and good works ascending through the heavens to the Throne, where they are heard making a buzzing noise resembling that of bees.

Mention should also be made of the speech of creatures that normally lack the faculty to express intelligible speech, like the dead, newborn babies, animals, birds, reptiles, insects, trees and shrubs, wood, stones, hills, and foodstuffs. Then there are the manifestations of such creatures' capacity to hear and understand human speech, while lacking the necessary apparatus either to hear or comprehend.

It is common knowledge among Muslims that the Prophet ﷺ hears those who greet him or invoke blessings upon him and that he answers them, but rare are the people who can hear his answer. However, such events have been historically documented with sufficient frequency to put the phenomenon beyond dispute.

The worlds of dream-visions, imagination, similitudes and unveiling are evidently closely interconnected, bearing more resemblance to each other than differences, forming what seems to be a continuum of subtle gradations. Thus, true dream-visions and sound imagination are nothing but intra-psychic extensions of the World of Similitudes. Unveiling reveals both that which is intra-psychic or subjective, and that which is extra-psychic, occurring in the objective outer space. Formless intelligible realities from the higher worlds appear in any of these dimensions as subtle forms, but also in solid forms when they appear in the physical world. In both cases, they may appear as clearly comprehensible images, or as symbols needing interpretation. The angels as well as the spirits are formless spiritual lights in the Spiritual World; they assume a subtle form in the subtle dimension and a solid physical form in the physical world.

A good example to illustrate the close similarity between the various subtle dimensions is the form in which this world appears in dream-visions, in the World of Similitudes, and in the Hereafter. The Follower al-ʿAlāʾ ibn Ziyād al-ʿAdawī, a student of the Companion Anas ibn Mālik,[i] had a symbolic vision of this world in a dream-vision. He said, "I saw in my dream the people following someone, so I followed along. I finally saw it to be an old woman, toothless, one-eyed, and bedecked in many ornaments. 'What are you?' I asked, to which she answered, 'I am the world.' I said, 'I ask God to make you hateful to me.' She replied, 'Yes, but only if you hate money.'"[400]

As for symbolic visions of this world in the waking state, let us quote the following episode. When the Prophet ﷺ set out on his Night Journey, he passed by an old woman standing by the side of the road. Later on when he asked Gabriel who she was, he was told, "There only remains life in this world as long as there remains life in this old woman."[401] The world appeared as an bedecked old woman to the Prophet ﷺ, firstly, because this is its reality – an ugly reality trying, in vain for those possessed of insight, to masquerade as a beauty – and (secondly) because of the reason stated by Gabriel, which is that the lifetime of humanity on this planet is drawing to its end. However, the Prophet ﷺ also saw another manifestation of this world on the same night, appearing as a woman extending her naked arms, dressed in every conceivable form of ornament, calling upon him, "O Muḥammad, look at me, allow me to ask you!" He never looked nor did he stop. When he asked Gabriel, he was told that this had been the world and that had he looked at her his community would have been seduced by it.[402]

Furthermore, we have numerous reports in the literature of this world appearing for various purposes to men of God. Imām Qushayrī, for example, reports that two of the great Sufis of Iraq, Abū ʿĀṣim al-Baṣrī and Sarī al-Saqatī, were seen to be served, at a certain stage in their lives, by an old woman who cleaned their lodgings and brought them their food when they broke their fast in the evening.[403] Another example is that of Shaykh ʿAbd al-Qādir al-Jīlānī, who said that during his days of strenuous asceticism the world used to take shape for

---

i Al-ʿAlāʾ ibn Ziyād al-ʿAdawī of Baṣra was a Follower who was an ascetic, a scholar and a transmitter of *ḥadīth* from Anas ibn Mālik, ʿAbdallāh ibn ʿUmar, ʿAbdallāh ibn ʿAmr, and other Companions. He died in 94 AH.

him, together with its ornaments and pleasures, but God protected him from it.[404] Finally, we have the description of Ibn ʿAbbās of how this world will appear on the Day of Resurrection. He said, "This world will be brought on the Day of Resurrection in the form of a grey-haired, dark-skinned, malformed old woman, with protruding fangs, standing above the people. They will be asked, 'Do you know this one?' They will answer, 'We ask God's protection against knowing this one!' They will be told, 'This is the world that you have fought each other for, ruptured your bonds of kinship for, envied and hated each other for, and deluded yourselves about.' Then it will be cast into the Fire and will call, 'Lord! Where are my followers and my allies?' God will say, 'Let her followers and allies join her!'"[405]

We have thus seen the world appear in a dream, in the waking state, and in the Hereafter in human forms whose descriptions are sometimes strikingly similar, when it is in reality an intelligible concept. Such forms need to be interpreted for the real meaning to appear, and this applies to the whole spectrum beginning with the worlds of dream-visions and similitudes in this life, to that of the Day of Resurrection in the next.

We are now able to conclude that the hidden dimensions of both man and the universe are much vaster and richer than their physical dimension; and that the higher the dimension the more important and real it becomes and capable of influencing the dimensions beneath it. Thus, in man, we find that each person's thoughts, beliefs and emotions control the activities of the body, while in the universe the subtle dimensions contain the realities of the physical world, and the formless spiritual dimension contains the realities of the formal subtle world. Ultimately, all these realities find their origins in the Divine knowledge. The more the soul is enlightened with the love, worship and remembrance of God, the more likely it is to penetrate the veils of the hidden dimensions and perceive some of their realities. The first level of this consists in true dream-visions, then the more powerful one's certainty becomes the more one's imagination becomes active and the closer one comes to achieving the Vision of Certainty. Then the eye of the heart opens and one sees images of these realities in the World of Similitudes, before finally reaching the level where the Opening becomes complete and one witnesses the highest worlds and the action of the Divine attributes in the universe.

Knowledge of the subtle dimensions is necessary to understand many passages of the Qur'ān, Prophetic *ḥadīth*s and the utterances and events in the lives of the men of God. We have already discussed this in Part Two with regard to *Sūra al-Takāthur* of the Qur'ān. We shall now examine one of the *ḥadīth*s describing the Ascension to demonstrate how a single *ḥadīth* may refer to different modes of manifestation of the World of Similitudes. The Prophet ﷺ said:

> *The roof of my house was split open in Makka and Gabriel descended. He split my chest open, washed it with Zamzam water, then brought a golden basin full of wisdom and faith, and emptied it into my chest, which he then closed. Then he took my hand and led me on an ascent toward Heaven. When he reached the Terrestrial Heaven, he said to the keeper, "Open!" To which he replied, "Who is this?" He said, "This is Gabriel." He asked, "Who is with you?" He replied, "With me is Muḥammad." He asked, "Was he sent for?" He said, "Yes, so open up." When we were above the Terrestrial Heaven there was a man to whose right was a crowd and to whose left was a crowd. When he looked to his right he laughed, but when he looked leftwards he wept. He said, "Welcome to the virtuous Prophet and virtuous son." I said, "Who is this, Gabriel?" He answered, "This is Adam, and the crowds on his right and left are his descendants. Those on the right are the people of the Garden and those on the left are the people of the Fire. Thus, when he looks right, he laughs; and when he looks left, he weeps." Then Gabriel took me up till he reached the Second Heaven and said to its keeper, "Open up!" He received the same answer, then it was opened.*

The Prophet ﷺ then stated that he found in the heavens Enoch (Idrīs), Moses, Jesus and Abraham. Then he said that he was taken up to a level where he heard the squeaking of the pens. Thereafter he was led to the Supreme Lotus, then to the Garden.[406]

The *ḥadīth* begins by the roof of the house being split open, which obviously did not happen in the material dimension. However, this was a higher reality that overruled the material reality by being more real. Gabriel then descended through the crack in the roof. He split the

Prophet's chest open, again not in the material dimension, but nevertheless a very real splitting. He then brought from the Unseen a basin filled with faith and wisdom, to pour them into the Prophet's open chest. Now faith and wisdom are both intelligible realities, possessing neither material nor subtle forms, but here they took on a form that could be seen by the Prophet ﷺ, although he did not describe them, so we cannot tell whether it was subtle or material. In this particular narration no mention is made of the Night Journey to Jerusalem and the events that took place there, but it goes straight away to the Ascension. In the *Malakūt*, the heavens have doors on which stand keepers, they ask questions and demand answers, then they open them to allow permitted visitors to enter. In each heaven are one or more Divine Envoys. These are all subtle forms, as are those of the Lotus of the Supreme Limit and the Garden.

Again, when the Prophet ﷺ says that on the Day of Judgement the disbelievers will be mustered on their faces, adding that He who has made them walk on their feet in this life will make them walk on their faces in the next,[407] we are now able to recognise that in the World of Similitudes this is quite possible. Similarly, when we are told about those who enjoin good but fail to do it and forbid evil yet do it, that their entrails will spill out on the ground in Hell and they will drag them around like a donkey turning a mill,[408] we will recognise that this again is a manifestation of the World of Similitudes in the Hereafter. This applies to the descriptions of life in both Heaven and Hell.

The Divine Decree descends from the World of the Divine Command, travelling down through the worlds, to manifest itself in the material dimension in the form of the events that occur there. This is described in the Qur'an as follows: ***God it is who created seven heavens and of the earth an equal number. His command descends through them, that you may know that God is able to do all things and that God encompasses everything in knowledge.***[409] And: ***He directs a command from heaven to earth, then it ascends to Him in a day that measures a thousand years of your reckoning.***[410] God may decide to reveal His decrees as they descend through the worlds to some of His beloved servants before they appear in the material world, and this may be done either in dream-visions or in waking visions of the World of Similitudes.

We have also learned from our inquiry that inner states (such as faith and disbelief, or knowledge and ignorance) and actions (such as recitations of various *sūras* of the Qur'ān, ritual prayers or *zakāt*) have a separate existence in the World of Similitudes. There they acquire a form that speaks and is spoken to, and is able to protect, intercede for or to the contrary damn their author. One can understand that as a person lives in this world, his inner and outer actions and experiences will shape his subtle psychological form, the form that will be taken to the grave at the time of death and constitute his intimate environment until the Day of Resurrection. This is how two contiguous graves may be so different that one of them is a meadow of Paradise and the other a pit of Hell. Just as, in this world, Prophets, saints and sacred places and times are loci for the descent of Divine lights and mercy – for like attracts like – so in the subtle world of the grave the soul of a virtuous man will attract lights and mercies upon himself and those surrounding him, while the soul of an evil man will attract shadows and wrath, but mainly if not entirely upon himself. For light has a much more powerful tendency to radiate than darkness. Proximity to the grave of a man of God will therefore be a source of mercy and blessings, while proximity to that of an evil man will be no more than an irritation to the believer.

The great majority of events quoted herein are from the life of the Prophet ﷺ, for these are accounts that have been meticulously authenticated by scholars of *ḥadīth*, so as to leave no room for denial or doubt. But if some of the narrow minds in our times should object that these occurrences are an exclusive prerogative of the Prophet ﷺ, we have added accounts of similar events in the lives of his Companions, then in those of the following generations of men of God up to the present day. We have included reports from thoroughly reliable contemporary sources to demonstrate that the pattern has continued in an uninterrupted form from the Prophet's days to ours and manifests immutable Divine laws.

We sometimes hear certain people raising the objection that if it were possible to see the Prophet ﷺ in full wakefulness and ask him about things, then why did not the Companions do so when they were in serious trouble? And if the fragrance of musk can be perceived at the tombs of some scholars and saints, then why was it not smelled from the tomb of the Prophet ﷺ and the Companions? Such objections aim at denying these phenomena altogether and accusing of dishonesty all the upright imāms who have reported them in their books over the centuries. Of course, the ultimate aim of such objections is simply to deny that Muslims have ever had saints or that there is such a thing as Sufism. Nonetheless, the answer to such protestations is that regardless of whether we know or not why these phenomena have been reported about some men but not others who are obviously superior, the phenomena in themselves are undeniable as they have been reported in overwhelming profusion.

One of the companions of Imām ʿAlī named Abu'l-Ṭufayl reported that he had seen ʿAlī preaching, saying, "Ask me, for by God, you shall ask me of nothing that is to be until the Day of Resurrection but that I shall tell you about it. Ask me about the Book of God, for by God, there is no verse in it but that I know whether it had been revealed by night or by day, in a plain or on a mountain." At that time, there was a man named Ibn al-Kawwāʾ, who had been one of the chief Khārijites before reverting to orthodoxy, accepting the authority of ʿAlī, and becoming one of his companions; he eventually became known for asking a great many questions. On that day, he stood up behind Abu'l-Ṭufayl, and asked, "Do you know what the Populous House (*Bayt al-Maʿmūr*) is?" ʿAlī answered, "That is the Parallel House (*Ḍurāḥ*) that is above the seven heavens, underneath the Throne. It is entered every day by seventy thousand angels who never return to it until the Day of Resurrection."[411] The point here is that ʿAlī could not possibly have made such a claim – in other words, be capable of answering any question at all – unless the Unseen had been clearly unveiled to him, as we expect it to have been for a man of such spiritual stature, as also for numerous others among the Companions.

The Prophet ﷺ said that there does not come a day without the grave saying, "I am the house of estrangement! I am the house of loneliness! I am the house of dust! I am the house of worms!" When the believing servant is buried, the grave says to him, "Welcome! I loved those who walked on my surface coming to me. Now that you have come to me and I have taken charge of you, you will see what I will do with you!" Then it enlarges as far as he can see and a door is opened for him onto Paradise. But when the disbelieving or corrupt servant is buried, the grave says to him, "You are not welcome! I hated those who walked on my surface coming to me. Now that you have come to me and I have taken charge of you, you will see what I will do with you!" Then it closes upon him until he is squeezed so much that his ribs are crushed together.[412] There are many things in this *ḥadīth* that can only be understood in terms of subtle forms, for they would be physically impossible in the material world. The inanimate grave speaks to the dead person in a tongue he can hear and understand, then it enlarges as far as he can see and a door opens from which he can see his place in Paradise; or it constricts and crushes him, and a door opens from which he can see his place in Hell. We have already been told that the grave is either a meadow of Paradise or a pit of Hell. Now were we to open the grave after a burial, we would see nothing of all this. Furthermore, there could be two contiguous graves, in one of which the dead person is enjoying the pleasure of Paradise, while in the other the dead person is suffering the pains of Hell; yet from the outside, they would both look exactly the same.

One must keep in mind that every creature has two aspects: one apparent and turned towards this world; and another hidden and turned towards God. The one turned towards God is what we call its reality. For instance, the material reality of trees and pebbles is well known, but their hidden realities are different, and they are possessed of consciousness and engaged in constant glorification of their Maker. God says in the Qur'ān, ***The seven heavens and the earth and those in them hymn His praises. There is nothing that does not hymn His praises, but you comprehend not their praises. He is Forbearing, Forgiving.***[413] Thus does each creature have a subtle reality that is in constant glorification of its Lord; but because it belongs to the hidden subtle dimension, it cannot be perceived by the ordinary physical senses, unless it manifests exceptionally in physical form. When it does it is considered a supernatural or miraculous event. Much of what is termed miraculous can be explained in terms of the *'Ālam al-Mithāl*. Powerful spirits such as Prophets and saints are not only able to perceive much of these dimensions, but also to render those around them able to perceive them as well under certain circumstances.

Another *ḥadīth* that would be difficult to understand without the concept of the subtle realities of the World of Similitudes is the one where shortly after sunset the Prophet ﷺ asked Abū Dharr about the sun: "*Do you know where it goes?*" The latter replied, "God and His Messenger know best." He said, "*It goes to prostrate itself beneath the Throne, at which time it asks permission and is granted it. Soon its prostration will not be accepted: it will ask permission and be refused it; and it will be told, 'Return from whence you came!' and it will rise from where it usually sets. This is His saying – exalted is He! –* ***And the sun runs to its resting place; that is the ordaining of the August, the Knowing.***"[414] We know that the sun is a formidable star swimming in space and that the earth revolves around it, so that sunrise and sunset depend on the movement of the earth, not that of the sun. The Throne, on the other hand, is an immeasurably more formidable sphere, not material but subtle and luminous, containing the whole created universe. It is therefore impossible for the material sun to prostrate itself before the immaterial Throne, but it is entirely possible for the sun's subtle reality to do so in the subtle dimension. It is this reality which can be said to speak and ask for permission and understand whether it is granted it or not. We should, then, remember that the higher worlds control and influence the lower, so that what happens in the subtle dimensions is then reflected in what happens in the material world. Thus, when it is refused permission, the forces regulating the solar system will be more or less disrupted to bring about a cataclysmic event of the order of the earth reversing its spin so that the sun appears to rise from the West.

It is obvious that these immense vibrant worlds that constitute the Unseen, although interpenetrating the material dimension, are in no way of the same substance, but differ from it in such an essential manner that they can never be captured using material technology, however advanced. Now in those instances when the unseen realities manifest in the material world, they take on the qualities of the material world. When they assume these qualities to the full, they become perceptible to the senses. When they assume them partly, then they can only be seen or heard by those who are spiritually qualified. This is how, as we have shown, the same angel that Divine envoys see and converse with in human form is often, but not always, neither seen nor heard by those around them. As for penetrating the Unseen, it can only be done through the spirit, either in dreams, which may happen to everyone, or in the waking state, which requires spiritual qualifications.

Knowledge of the unseen dimensions is essential to place into perspective the importance of all that is happening on this planet in terms of scientific progress and technology. Only this knowledge is capable of protecting Muslim minds from contamination by the materialistic attitudes of the modern world. We must remember that the material dimension is no more than a speck of dust compared to the immensity of the worlds of subtle images, which are in turn even smaller when compared to the worlds of spiritual lights. The real life of the human being can never be contained by the material dimension, for the real purpose of his existence is spiritual. Therefore, confining one's horizon and interests to material and social pleasures means that the real purpose of human existence, which is precisely knowledge of the Unseen, will be missed. This knowledge, as is well known to the Muslims, has three levels: the first being mental knowledge; the second is vision at a distance with the inner eye of the heart; and the third is the intimate experience of the Unseen, which is termed the Truth of Certainty. Again, all three levels start with the created Unseen, the World of Similitudes, then with the uncreated Unseen, the World of Divine Attributes. Indeed, the ultimate and only worthwhile goal for a human being is to be admitted to the Presence of the Real.

Endnotes

1. Ṭabarānī, *Awsaṭ*, 5378.
2. Qur'ān, *Sūra Fāṭir*, 35:1.
3. Muslim, *Muslim, Ṣaḥīḥ: kitāb al-fitan wa ashrāṭ al-sāʿa, bāb dhikr al-Dajjāl wa ṣifatih wa mā maʿah, 5228*, 5228.
4. Qur'ān, *Sūra al-Fatḥ*, 48:4.
5. Muslim, *Ṣaḥīḥ: kitāb al-dhikr wa'l-duʿā' wa'l-tawba wa'l-istighfār, bāb faḍl al-ijtimāʿ ʿalā tilāwat al-Qur'ān wa ʿalā al-dhikr*, 4867–68.
6. Abū Dāwūd, *Sunan: kitāb al-jihād, bāb fi'l-rukhṣa fi'l-quʿūd min al-ʿudhr*, 2146.
7. Aḥmad, *Musnad*, 793.
8. Bukhārī, *Ṣaḥīḥ: kitāb faḍā'il aṣḥāb al-Nabī, bāb manāqib ʿUmar ibn al-Khaṭṭāb, 3689; Muslim, Ṣaḥīḥ: kitāb faḍā'il al-Ṣaḥāba, bāb min faḍā'il ʿUmar*, 2398.
9. Al-Ḥākim, *Mustadrak*, 3014.
10. Abū Nuʿaym al-Aṣbahānī, *Dalā'il al-Nubuwwa*, 538.
11. Ibn Ḥibbān, *Ṣaḥīḥ*, 6510; Dārimī, *Sunan*, 13; Aḥmad, *Musnad*, 16525, 16537, 16990; Ṭabarānī, *Kabīr*, 15032–33; al-Ḥākim, *Mustadrak*, 3525, 4140, 4196; Bayhaqī, *Shuʿab al-Īmān*, 1374.
12. Bayhaqī, *Dalā'il al-Nubuwwa*, 29.
13. Aḥmad, *Musnad*, 1963.
14. Aḥmad, *Musnad*, 8286, 8402.
15. Muslim, *Ṣaḥīḥ: kitāb al-ru'yā, 4200; Abū Dāwūd, Sunan: kitāb al-adab, bāb mā jā' fi'l-ru'yā*, 4365.
16. Ibn Māja, *Sunan: bāb man laʿib bih al-Shayṭān fī manāmih fa lā yuḥaddith bih al-nās*, 3902.
17. Abū Dāwūd, *Sunan: kitāb al-adab, bāb fi'l-waqār*, 4146.
18. ʿAbd al-Razzāq, *Muṣannaf*, 7610.
19. Bukhārī, *Ṣaḥīḥ: kitāb al-janā'iz, bāb mā qīl fī awlād al-mushrikīn*, 1386.
20. Bukhārī, *Ṣaḥīḥ: kitāb al-ru'yā, bāb mā jā' fī taʿbīr al-ru'yā*, 2278–80.
21. Tirmidhī, *Sunan, kitāb al-ru'yā, bāb mā jā' fī taʿbīr al-ru'yā*, 2278–80.
22. Dārimī, *Sunan*, 2218.

23. Rāzī, *Tafsīr*, 13:142.
24. Qur'ān, *Sūra al-Ṣāffāt*, 37:99–102.
25. Qur'ān, *Sūra al-Anfāl*, 8:43–44.
26. Bukhārī, *Ṣaḥīḥ: kitāb al-manāqib, bāb 'alāmāt al-nubuwwa fi'l-Islām*, 3622.
27. Aḥmad, *Musnad, Musnad Jābir ibn 'Abdallāh*, 14260.
28. Bukhārī, *Ṣaḥīḥ: kitāb al-manāqib, bāb 'alāmāt al-nubuwwa fi'l-Islām*, 3621.
29. Bukhārī, *Ṣaḥīḥ: kitāb al-manāqib, bāb manāqib 'Umar ibn al-Khaṭṭāb*, 3691.
30. Bukhārī, *Ṣaḥīḥ: kitāb al-manāqib, bāb manāqib 'Umar ibn al-Khaṭṭāb*, 3681.
31. Bukhārī, *Ṣaḥīḥ: kitāb al-ta'bīr, bāb al-mar'a al-sawdā'*, 7038–40.
32. 'Abd al-Razzāq, *Muṣannaf*, 5559–60.
33. Aḥmad ibn Ḥanbal, *Kitāb al-Zuhd*, 2399.
34. Qurṭubī, *Tafsīr, Sūra al-Najm*, 17:110; Daylamī, *Musnad al-Firdaws*, 6519.
35. Aḥmad, *Musnad: Musnad Jābir ibn 'Abdallāh*, 14750.
36. Bukhārī, *Ṣaḥīḥ: kitāb al-ṭibb, bāb man lam yurq*, 5752.
37. Bukhārī, *Ṣaḥīḥ: kitāb al-ta'bīr, bāb man lam yarā al-ru'yā li awwal 'ābir idhā lam yuṣib*, 7046.
38. Aḥmad, *Musnad*, 15881, 21018.
39. Al-Ḥākim, *Mustadrak*, 4374, 8307.
40. Bukhārī, *Ṣaḥīḥ: kitāb al-tahajjud, bāb faḍl qiyām al-layl*, 1121–22.
41. Bukhārī, *Ṣaḥīḥ: kitāb manāqib al-Anṣār, bāb manāqib 'Abdallāh ibn Salām*, 3813.
42. Abū Dāwūd, *Sunan: kitāb al-Sunna, bāb fi'l-khulafā'*, 4017.
43. Bukhārī, *Ṣaḥīḥ: kitāb al-ta'bīr, bāb man ra'ā al-Nabī fi'l-manām*, 6993.
44. Bukhārī, *Ṣaḥīḥ: kitāb al-ta'bīr, bāb man ra'ā al-Nabī fi'l-manām*, 6697.
45. Ibn 'Asākir, *Tārīkh Dimashq*, 5:311–12; Ibn Kathīr, *al-Bidāya wa'l-Nihāya*, 10:365.
46. Ibn 'Asākir, *Tārīkh Dimashq*, 5:311–12; Dhahabī, *Tadhkirat al-Ḥuffāẓ*, 3:975.
47. Tirmidhī, *Sunan: kitāb tafsīr al-Qur'ān, Sūra Ṣād*, 3233–35; Dārimī, *Sunan: kitāb al-ru'yā, bāb fī ru'yat al-Rabb ta'ālā fi'l-nawm*, 2149.
48. Muslim, *Ṣaḥīḥ: kitāb al-masājid, bāb al-nahi min akl thawm…*, 567; Aḥmad, *Musnad: Musnad 'Umar ibn al-Khaṭṭāb*, 85; al-Ḥākim, *Mustadrak: kitāb ma'rifat al-Ṣaḥāba, maqtal 'Umar*, 4510.
49. Ṭabarānī, *Awsaṭ*, 7463.
50. Ibn Abī Shayba, *Muṣannaf: kitāb al-Īmān wa'l-ru'yā*, 7:244.
51. Qur'ān, *Sūra Quraysh*, 102.
52. Ibn Abī Shayba, *Muṣannaf*: 30425; Bazzār, *Kashf al-Astār*, 32; Ṭabarānī, *Kabīr*, 3367; Bayhaqī, *Shu'ab al-Īmān*, 10106–7.
53. Muslim, *Ṣaḥīḥ: kitāb al-tawba, bāb faḍl dawām al-dhikr wa'l-fikr fī umūr al-*

ākhira, 275.

54. Ibn Saʿd, *Ṭabaqāt*, 4:167; Ibn ʿAsākir, *Tārīkh Dimashq*, 40:271; Fākihī, *Akhbār Makka*, 320.
55. Bukhārī, *Ṣaḥīḥ: kitāb al-ṣalāt, bāb ḥakk al-buzāq bi'l-yadd min al-masjid*, 406.
56. Bukhārī, *Ṣaḥīḥ: kitāb al-Īmān, bāb su'āl Jibrīl al-Nabī ṣalla'llāhu alayhi wa sallam ʿan al-Īmān wa'l-Islām wa'l-Iḥsān, wa ʿilm al-sāʿa*, 50.
57. Tirmidhī, *Sunan: kitāb al-tafsīr, bāb wa min sūrat idhā'l-shams kuwwirat*, 3333. The *sūras* referred to are *sūras* 81, 82 and 84.
58. Bukhārī, *Ṣaḥīḥ: kitāb al-maghāzī, bāb Ghazwat Uḥud*, 4049.
59. Muslim, *Ṣaḥīḥ: kitāb al-zuhd wa'l-raqā'iq, bāb fī aḥādīth mutafarriqa*, 2996.
60. Qur'ān, *Sūra al-ʿAlaq*, 96:1-3.'
61. Bukhārī, *Ṣaḥīḥ: kitāb bad' al-khalq, bāb dhikr al-malā'ika*, 3238.
62. Bukhārī, *Ṣaḥīḥ: kitāb bad' al-waḥī*, 3.
63. Bukhārī, *Ṣaḥīḥ: kitāb bad' al-khalq, bāb idhā qāl aḥadukum Āmīn!* 3232.
64. Bukhārī, *Ṣaḥīḥ: kitāb bad' al-khalq, bāb dhikr al-malā'ika*, 3231; Muslim, *Ṣaḥīḥ: kitāb al-jihād wa'l-siyar, bāb mā laqiya al-Nabī ṣalla Allāh ʿalayh wa sallam min adhā al-mushrikīn wa'l-Munāfiqīn*, 3352.
65. Ṭabarānī, *Kabīr*, 11893.
66. Ibn Ḥibbān, *Ṣaḥīḥ: dhikr Ḥanẓala ibn Abī ʿĀmir Ghasīl al-malā'ika riḍwān Allāh ʿalayh*, 7151.
67. Ibn Hishām, *Sīra*, 1:188.
68. Al-Ḥākim. *Mustadrak: kitāb al-tafsīr, tafsīr Sūra al-Taḥrīm*, 3834.
69. Bukhārī, *Ṣaḥīḥ: kitāb bad' al-khalq, bāb dhikr al-malā'ika*, 3217.
70. Qur'ān, *Sūra Maryam*, 19:16–17.
71. Bukhārī, *Ṣaḥīḥ: kitāb aḥādīth al-Anbiyā', bāb yazzifūn*, 3364; Azraqī, *Akhbār Makka*, 47.
72. Genesis, 16:7–11, King James Bible.
73. Muslim, *Ṣaḥīḥ: kitāb al-Īmān, bāb bayān al-Īmān wa'l-Islām wa'l-Iḥsān*, 9; Tirmidhī, *Sunan: kitāb al-Īmān, bāb mā jā' fī wasf Jibrīl li'l-Nabī al-Īmān wa'l-Islām*, 2535.
74. Aḥmad, *Musnad*, 23945; al-Ḥākim, *Mustadrak*, 4301.
75. Bukhārī, *Ṣaḥīḥ: kitāb al-maghāzī, bāb marjiʿ al-Nabī ṣalla Allāh ʿalayh wa sallam min al-aḥzāb wa makhrajih ilā Banī Qurayẓa*, 4119.
76. Aḥmad, *Musnad*, 448; ʿAbd al-Razzāq, *Muṣannaf*, 20545; Ṭabarānī, *Kabīr*, 3152.
77. Aḥmad, *Musnad*, 19459, 22014.
78. Al-Ḥākim, *Mustadrak: kitāb maʿrifat al-Ṣaḥāba*,, 6722.
79. Bukhārī, *al-Adab al-Mufrad: bāb shikāyat al-jār*, 126; Ibn Ḥajar al-ʿAsqalānī,

al-Maṭālib al-ʿĀliya, 2820; Ṭabarānī, *Kabīr*, 15864.

80. Ibn Māja, *Sunan: kitāb al-adab, bāb faḍl al-Ḥāmidīn*, 3791.
81. Aḥmad, *Musnad*, 22266.
82. Tirmidhī, *Sunan: kitāb al-manāqib, bāb manāqib Saʿd ibn Muʿādh*, 3849.
83. Bukhārī, *Ṣaḥīḥ: kitāb bad' al-khalq, bāb dhikr al-malāʾika*, 3211.
84. Ibn Ḥibbān, *Ṣaḥīḥ*, 3398; Bayhaqī, *Shuʿab al-Īmān*, 9986.
85. Muslim, *Ṣaḥīḥ: kitāb al-masājid, bāb mā yuqāl bayn takbirat wa'l-iḥrām wa'l-qirāʾa*, 600.
86. ʿAbd al-Razzāq, *Muṣannaf*, 19990.
87. Wāqidī, *Maghāzī*, 1:75–76.
88. Tirmidhī, *Sunan: kitāb al-manāqib, bāb manāqib Saʿd ibn Muʿādh*, 3849.
89. Bayhaqī, *al-Sunan al-Kubrā*, 6:168.
90. Qur'ān, *Sūra Hūd*, 11:69–70.
91. Qur'ān, *Sūra al-Ḥijr*, 15:61–62.
92. Muslim, *Ṣaḥīḥ: kitāb al-birr wa'l-ṣila wa'l-adab, bāb fī faḍl al-ḥubb fi'llāh*, 2567.
93. Muslim, *Ṣaḥīḥ: kitāb al-tawba, bāb faḍl dawām al-dhikr wa'l-fikr fī umūr al-ākhira wa'l-murāqaba*, 2750.
94. Lālikāʾī, *Sharḥ Uṣūl Iʿtiqād Ahl al-Sunna wa'l-Jamāʿa*, 2433.
95. Qur'ān, *Sūra Fuṣṣilat*, 41:30–31.
96. Ibn Hishām, *Sīra*, 1:632; Bayhaqī, *Dalāʾil al-Nubuwwa*, 901.
97. Al-Ḥākim, *Mustadrak: kitāb maʿrifat al-Ṣaḥāba*, 4431; Bayhaqī, *Dalāʾil al-Nubuwwa*, 906.
98. Bukhārī, *Ṣaḥīḥ: kitāb al-maghāzī, bāb idh hammat ṭāʾifatān minkum an tafshalā*, 4055.
99. Wāqidī, *Maghāzī*, 1:79; Bayhaqī, *Dalāʾil al-Nubuwwa*, 916.
100. Ibn al-Qayyim, *al-Rūḥ*, (Cairo: Dār al-Manār, 1419/1999), 71.
101. Ibn Ḥajar al-Haytamī, *al-Ḍurr al-Manḍūd fi'l-Ṣalāt wa'l-Salām ʿalā Ṣāḥib al-Maqām al-Maḥmūd*, (Madina: Dār al-Madīna al-Munawwara lil-nashr wa'l-tawzīʿ, 1416/1995).
102. Abu'l-Qāsim ʿAbd al-Karīm al-Qushayrī, *al-Risāla al-Qushayriyya fī ʿIlm al-Taṣawwuf*, (Cairo: Maktabat wa Maṭbaʿat Muḥammad ʿAlī Ṣubayḥ wa Awlāduh, 1392/1972).
103. Ibn Ḥajar al-Haytamī, *al-Ḍurr al-Manḍūd*, 136.
104. Tirmidhī, *Sunan: kitāb tafsīr al-Qur'ān, bāb Sūra al-Aʿrāf*, 3075.
105. Aḥmad, *Musnad: Musnad Abī Hurayra*, 9063.
106. Ṭabarānī, *Awsaṭ*, 7479.
107. Ibn Abī Ḥātim, *Tafsīr*, 2730.
108. Aḥmad, *Kitāb al-Zuhd*, 229.

109. Ṭabarānī, *Kabīr*, 4075; Ibn Abī ʿĀṣim, *al-Āḥad wa'l-Mathānī*, 1989.
110. Ṭabarānī, *Kabīr*, 2821; Bayhaqī, *Dalā'il al-Nubuwwa*, 3250.
111. Abū Nuʿaym al-Aṣbahānī, *Maʿrifat al-Ṣaḥāba*, 464.
112. Ṭabarī, *Tafsīr*, 19:69; Qur'ān, *Sūra al-Mu'minūn*, 23:99–100.
113. Qushayrī, *Risāla*, 43.
114. Al-Ḥākim, *Mustadrak*, 292; Ṭabarānī, *Kabīr*, 10429–30; Fākihī, *Akhbār Makka*, 1569. The verse is from *Sūra al-Fajr*, 89:27.
115. Wāmiq al-Dīn Aydīn al-Firsāfī, *Ḥayāt al-Shaykh Muḥammad al-Ḥazīn al-Firsāfī wa Manāqibuh*, published by the author, undated, 19.
116. Bukhārī, *Ṣaḥīḥ: kitāb faḍā'il al-Qur'ān, bāb nuzūl al-sakīna wa'l-malā'ika ʿind qirā'at al-Qur'ān*, 5018.
117. Abū Dāwūd, *Sunan: kitāb qirā'at al-Qur'ān, bāb fī thawāb qirā'at al-Qur'ān*, 1243.
118. Ibn ʿAṭā'illāh al-Iskandarī, *Laṭā'if al-Minan*, edited by Shaykh ʿAbd al-Ḥalīm Maḥmūd, Cairo, 224.
119. Ṭabarānī, *Awsaṭ*, 7135.
120. Al-Ḥākim, *Mustadrak: kitāb al-tafsīr, tafsīr Sūra Āl ʿImrān*, 3154.
121. Bukhārī, *Ṣaḥīḥ: kitāb aḥādīth al-Anbiyā', bāb qawl Allāh taʿālā: wa hal atāka ḥadīth Mūsā*, 3394; Muslim, *Ṣaḥīḥ: kitāb al-Īmān, bāb al-Isrā' bi Rasūl Allāh*, 239–240.
122. Muslim, *Ṣaḥīḥ: kitāb al-faḍā'il, bāb min faḍā'il Mūsā*, 2375; *kitāb qiyām al-layl wa taṭawwuʿ al-nahār, bāb dhikr ṣalāt Nabī Allāh Mūsā*, 1613.
123. Aḥmad, *Musnad*, 3365; Abū Yaʿlā, *Musnad*, 2659.
124. Muslim, *Ṣaḥīḥ: kitāb al-Īmān, bāb al-Isrā' bi Rasūl Allāh ilā al-samāwāt*, 243.
125. Ṭabarānī, *Kabīr*, 12283.
126. Muslim, *Ṣaḥīḥ: kitāb al-Īmān, bāb al-Isrā' bi Rasūl Allāh*, 268–69.
127. Al-Najm al-Ghazzī, *al-Kawākib al-Sā'ira bi A'yān al-Mā'a al-ʿĀshira*, 1:144.
128. Shaʿrānī, *al-Ṭabaqāt al-Kubrā*, (Beirut: Dār al-Jīl, 1408/1988).
129. Shaʿrānī, *al-Ṭabaqāt al-Ṣughrā*, (Cairo: Maktabat al-Qāhira, 1390/1970).
130. Ibid. 28.
131. Ṣāliḥ al-Jaʿfarī, *al-Muntaqā al-Nafīs*, Cairo, 1394/1975.
132. Yūsuf ibn Ismāʿīl al-Nabhānī, *Jāmiʿ Karāmāt al-Awliyā'*, (Cairo: Muṣṭafā al-Bābī al-Ḥalabī wa Awlāduh, 1404/1984).
133. Al-Firsāfī, *Ḥayāt al-Shaykh Muḥammad al-Ḥazīn al-Firsāfī*, 18.
134. Al-Firsāfī, *Ḥayāt al-Shaykh Muḥammad al-Ḥazīn al-Firsāfī*, 25.
135. Aḥmad Muḥammad Ḥijāb, *Al-ʿIẓa wa'l-Iʿtibār*, 120.
136. Ibid. 113.
137. Ṭāriq al-Sharīf, *Laṭā'if Rabbāniyya*, handwritten memoirs.

138. Ibn Qayyim al-Jawziyya, *al-Rūḥ*, 9. Muṭarrif is a Follower and transmitter of *ḥadīth* who died between 133 and 142 AH.
139. Ibn Qayyim al-Jawziyya, *al-Rūḥ*, 72–73.
140. Al-Iskandarī, *Laṭā'if al-Minan*, 226.
141. ʿAlī ibn ʿAbd al-Raḥmān al-Mashhūr, *Sharḥ al-Ṣudūr*, (Tarīm: Dār al-Uṣūl, undated), 194.
142. Mark, 9:2–4.
143. ʿAbd al-Qādir ibn Muḥyī al-Dīn al-Arbīlī, *Tafrīj al-Khāṭir*, 37.
144. Jūda Muḥammad Abu'l-Yazīd al-Mahdī, *Ḥaqīqat al-Qutb al-Nabawī al-Sayyid Aḥmad al-Badawī*, (Cairo: Dār Jawāmiʿ al-Kalim, 1425/2004), 380.
145. Muḥammad ibn Abū Bakr al-Shillī Bā-ʿAlawī, *al-Mashraʿ al-Rawī fī Manāqib al-Sāda al-Kirām Āl Abī Alawī*, Cairo, undated, 2:63–64.
146. Verbal communication from Dr. Sharīf ʿIssām, anaesthesiologist. 4 July 2012 CE.
147. Al-Mashhūr, *Sharḥ al-Ṣudūr*, 120–21.
148. Ibn Hishām, *Sīra*, 1:155, 156, 157; Bayhaqī, *Dalā'il al-Nubuwwa*, 22.
149. Bayhaqī, *Dalā'il al-Nubuwwa: bāb qiṣṣat'al-Ṭufayl ibn Amr al-Dawsī*, 2108.
150. Bukhārī, *Ṣaḥīḥ: kitāb manāqib al-Anṣār, bāb manqabat Usayd ibn Ḥuḍayr wa ʿAbbād ibn Bishr*, 3805.
151. Bayhaqī, *Dalā'il al-Nubuwwa*, 2330; al-Ḥākim, *Mustadrak: dhikr manāqib ʿAbdallāh Abī ʿAbs ibn Jabr al-Anṣārī al-Khazrajī*, 5495.
152. Ibn Abi'l-Dunyā, *Man ʿĀsha Baʿd al-Mawt*, 38.
153. Al-Ḥākim, *Mustadrak: kitāb al-maghāzī wa'l-sarāya*, 4391; Ṭabarānī, *Kabīr*, 2821; Bayhaqī, *Dalā'il al- Nubuwwa*, 3250–51.
154. Abū Dāwūd, *Sunan: kitāb al-janā'iz, bāb fī satr al-mayyit ʿind ghaslih*, 2733.
155. Aḥmad, *Musnad*, 18999; Bayhaqī, *al-Sunan al-Kubrā*, 5:14.
156. Bayhaqī, *Dalā'il al-Nubuwwa*, 3009.
157. Muslim, *Ṣaḥīḥ: kitāb al-ḥajj, bāb jawāz al-tamattuʿ*, 1226.
158. Aḥmad, *Musnad*, 1639; Ṭabarānī, *Kabīr*, 22266.
159. Ibn Abi'l-Dunyā, *Hawātif al-Jinān*, 11.
160. ʿAbd al-Razzāq, *Muṣannaf*, 4905; Ṭabarānī, *Kabīr*, 9353.
161. Abū Nuʿaym, *Ḥilyat al-Awliyā'*, 3:425.
162. Ibn Abi'l-Dunyā, *Hawātif al-Jinān*, 1:43.
163. Ibn Baṭṭa, *al-Ibāna al-Kubrā*, 2413.
164. Qushayrī, *Risāla*, 1:301.
165. Nabhānī, *Jāmiʿ Karāmāt al-Awliyā'*, 2:51.
166. Abū Dāwūd, *Sunan: kitāb al-Sunna, bāb fi'l-Qur'ān*, 4113.

167. Bukhārī, *Ṣaḥīḥ: kitāb bad' al-waḥī*, 2; Muslim, *Ṣaḥīḥ: kitāb al-faḍā'il, bāb 'araq al-Nabī ṣalla'llāh 'alayh wa sallam fi'l-bard wa ḥīn ya'tīh al-waḥī*, 4304.
168. Ṭabarānī, *Kabīr*, 3056; Awsaṭ, 11151; Bayhaqī, *Dalā'il al-Nubuwwa*, 938.
169. Aḥmad, *Musnad*, 21430; Ṭabarānī, *Kabīr*, 18192; Bayhaqī, *Dalā'il al-Nubuwwa*, 1894.
170. Muslim, *Ṣaḥīḥ: kitāb al-Janna, bāb fī shiddat ḥarr nār jahannam,*, 2844.
171. Muslim, *Ṣaḥīḥ: kitāb ṣifat al-Qiyāma wa'l-Janna wa'l-Nar, bāb qawluh inn al-insān layaṭghā, an ra'āh istaghnā*, 5005; Ibn Ḥibbān, *Ṣaḥīḥ*, 6691.
172. Al-Ḥārith ibn Usāma, *Musnad*, 383; Ibn Ḥajar al-'Asqalānī, *al-Maṭālib al-'Āliya*, 4328.
173. Azraqī, *Akhbār Makka*, 10–11, 13, 16, 23, 25, 40; Ṭabarī, *Tārīkh al-Rusul wa'l-Mulūk*, 1:43; 'Abd al-Razzāq, Muṣannaf: bāb bunyān al-Ka'ba, 9090.
174. Sha'rānī, *al-Ṭabaqāt al-Kubrā*, 2:104.
175. Tirmidhī, *Sunan: kitāb tafsīr al-Qur'ān, bāb Sūra al-A'rāf*, 3075.
176. Ibn Ḥibbān, *al-Thiqāt and Mashāhīr 'Ulamā' al-Amsār*; Abū Nu'aym, *Ḥilyat al-Awliyā'*, Dhahabī, *Tārīkh al-Islām*; Ibn al-Jawzī, *Ṣifat al-Ṣafwa*.
177. Ibn Ḥajar al-'Asqalānī, Introduction to *Fatḥ al-Bārī*, 1:494–95; Dhahabī, *Siyar A'lām al-Nubalā'*, 12:466.
178. Bukhārī, *Ṣaḥīḥ: kitāb al-adhān, bāb mā yaqūl ba'd al-takbīr*, 745; Muslim, *Ṣaḥīḥ: kitāb al-kusūf, bāb ṣalāt al-kusūf*, 1500; *bāb mā 'uriḍ 'alā al-Nabī ṣalla Allāh 'alayh wa sallam fī ṣalāt al-kusūf min amr al-Janna wa'l-Nār*, 1507.
179. Bukhārī, *Ṣaḥīḥ: kitāb al-jihād wa'l-siyar, bāb hal yasta'sir al-rajul*, 3045.
180. Aḥmad, *Musnad*, 22545; Bayhaqī, *Dalā'il al-Nubuwwa*, 2437–38.
181. Qur'ān, *Sūra al-Mā'ida*, 5:113–14.
182. Qur'ān, *Sūra Āl 'Imrān*, 3:37.
183. Ibid.
184. Bukhārī, *Ṣaḥīḥ: kitāb al-manāqib, bāb 'alāmāt al-nubuwwa fi'l-Islām*, 3572.
185. Ibid. 3573.
186. Ibid. 3581.
187. 'Abd al-Razzāq, *Muṣannaf*, 7900; Ibn Ḥajar al-'Asqalānī, *al-Iṣāba fī Ma'rifat al-Ṣaḥāba*, 4:77 and *al-Maṭālib al-'āliya*, 4225; Abū Nu'aym, *Ḥilyat al-Awliyā'*, 1:231; Ibn 'Asākir, *Tārīkh Dimashq*, 40:25, 8064.
188. Abū Nu'aym, *Ḥilyat al-Awliyā'*, 1:231; Ibn Ḥajar al-'Asqalānī, *al-Iṣāba fī Ma'rifat al-Ṣaḥāba*, 4:101; Ibn al-Jawzī, *al-Muntaẓim*, 2:156.
189. Ibn Qayyim al-Jawziyya, *al-Rūḥ*, 196.
190. Ibn Shāhin, *al-Targhīb fī Faḍā'il al-A'māl*, 32.
191. Ibn Ḥajar al-'Asqalānī, *al-Iṣāba fī Ma'rifat al-Ṣaḥāba*, 2:145, 146; Aḥmad ibn Ḥanbal, *Faḍā'il al-Ṣaḥāba*, 1890.

192. Ibn al-Qayyim, *al-Rūḥ*, 196.
193. ʿAbdallāh ibn Asʿad al-Yafiʿī, *Rawḍ al-Rayāḥīn fi Ḥikāyāt al-Ṣāliḥīn*, (Cairo: al-Maṭbaʿa al-Maymaniyya, 1307 AH).
194. Muslim, *Ṣaḥīḥ: kitāb al-Īmān, bāb dhikr al-Masīḥ ibn Maryam wa'l-Masīḥ al-Dajjāl*, 273–4.
195. Aḥmad, *Musnad*, 2680. ʿAqīl is the Prophet's cousin and ʿAlī's brother. He had a house not far from the Kaʿba.
196. Muslim, *Ṣaḥīḥ*, 172; Tabarānī, Awsat, 3879.
197. Bukhārī, *Ṣaḥīḥ: kitāb al-manāqib, bāb ʿalāmāt al-nubuwwa fi'l-Islām*, 3597.
198. Bukhārī, *Ṣaḥīḥ: kitāb al-ḥajj, bāb hadm al-Kaʿba*, 1595–96.
199. Bukhārī, *Ṣaḥīḥ: kitāb al-janā'iz, bāb al-ṣalāt ʿala'l-shahīd*, 1344.
200. Tirmidhī, *Sunan: kitāb ṣifat al-Qiyāma wa'l-raqā'iq wa'l-waraʿ*, 2492.
201. Bukhārī, *Ṣaḥīḥ: kitāb al-Īmān, bāb tafāḍul ahl al-Īmān fi'l-aʿmāl*, 12.
202. Tirmidhī, *Sunan: kitāb tafsīr al-Qur'ān, bāb wa min Sūra Banī Isrā'īl*, 3136.
203. Muslim, *Ṣaḥīḥ: kitāb ṣalāt al-musāfirīn wa qasrihā, bāb fadl qirā'at'al-Qur'ān wa Sūra al-Baqara*, 804.
204. Aḥmad, *Musnad*, 6337; al-Ḥākim, *Mustadrak: akhbār fi faḍā'il al-Qur'ān jumla*, 1994.
205. Bukhārī, *Ṣaḥīḥ: kitāb tafsīr al-Qur'ān, bāb qawlih: Yawm yukshaf ʿan sāq*, 4919.
206. ʿAbd al-Razzāq, *Muṣannaf*, 6001; Aḥmad, *Musnad*, 20318; Bayhaqī, *Shuʿab al-Īmān*, 2294.
207. Bukhārī, *Ṣaḥīḥ: kitāb tafsīr al-Qur'ān, bāb qawlih: Wa andhirhum yawm al-ḥasra*, 4730; Muslim, *Ṣaḥīḥ: kitāb al-Janna wa ṣifat naʿīmahā wa ahlahā, bāb al-Nār yadkhuluhā al-jabbārūn wa'l-Janna yadkhuluhā al-ḍuʿafā'*, 2849. The verse is from *Sūra Maryam*, 19:39.
208. Bukhārī, *Ṣaḥīḥ: kitāb al-zakāt, bāb ithm māniʿ al-zakāt*, 1337.
209. Tirmidhī, *Sunan: kitāb ṣifat al-Janna, bāb mā jā' fi sūq al-Janna*, 2550.
210. Bukhārī, *Ṣaḥīḥ: kitāb al-wuḍū', bāb faḍl al-wuḍū'*, 136.
211. Al-Ḥākim, *Mustadrak: kitāb al-tafsīr*, 3744. The Qur'ānic quotation is from *Sūra al-Ḥadīd*, 57:12.
212. Ṭabarānī, *Kabīr*, 9647.
213. Ibid. 7682.
214. Al-Ḥākim, *Mustadrak: tafsīr Sūra al-Ḥajj*, 3421; Ibn Ḥajar al-ʿAsqalānī, *al-Maṭālib al-ʿĀliya*, 1175.
215. Abū Nuʿaym, *Dalā'il al-Nubuwwa*, 509–12; Ṭabarī, *Tārīkh*, 3:254–55; Ibn al-Athīr, *Usd al-Ghāba*, 1:408.
216. Qur'ān, *Sūra Saba'*, 34:12.

217. Tirmidhī, *Sunan: kitāb al-amthāl, bāb mā jā' fī mathal Allāh li 'ibādih*, 2861.
218. Bukhārī, *Ṣaḥīḥ: kitāb al-tahajjud, bāb qiyām al-Nabī bi'l-layl fī Ramaḍān wa ghayrih*, 1147.
219. Bayhaqī, *Shu'ab al-Īmān*, 3923; al-Ḥākim, *Mustadrak*, 1666.
220. Ibn Khuzayma, *Ṣaḥīḥ: kitāb al-ḥajj, bāb bad' ramī al-Nabī al-jimār*, 2738; al-Ḥākim, *Mustadrak*, 1709.
221. Abū Nu'aym, *Ḥilyat al-Awliyā'*, 2:95.
222. 'Abd al-Razzāq, *Muṣannaf*, 20070.
223. Ghazālī, *Iḥyā'*, 2:409.
224. Matthew, 4:1–11; Luke, 4:1–13.
225. Nasā'ī, *Sunan: kitāb al-imāma, bāb ḥath al-imām 'alā raṣṣ al-ṣufūf*, 806.
226. Bukhārī, *Ṣaḥīḥ: kitāb al-ṣalāt, bāb al-asīr aw al-gharīm yurbaṭ fi'l-masjid*, 461. The verse is in Qur'ān, *Sūra Ṣād*, 38:35.
227. Aḥmad, *Musnad*, 8286, 8402.
228. Abū Ya'lā, *Musnad*, 4188; Bayhaqī, *Shu'ab al-Īmān*, 536.
229. Bukhārī, *Ṣaḥīḥ: kitāb faḍā'il Aṣḥāb al-Nabī, bāb manāqib 'Umar ibn al-Khaṭṭāb*, 3683.
230. Bukhārī, *Ṣaḥīḥ: kitāb al-wikāla, bāb idhā wakkal rajul fatarak al-wakīl shay'an*, 2311.
231. Ibn Hishām, *Sīra*, 1:480–81; Ibn Abī Ḥātim, *Tafsīr*, 9743.
232. Bayhaqī, *Dalā'il al-Nubuwwa*, 936, 971; Ibn Hishām, *Sīra*, 1:611; Ibn Abī Ḥātim, *Tafsīr*, 9908.
233. Sha'rānī, *al-Ṭabaqāt al-Kubrā*, 1:85.
234. Muḥammad ibn Yaḥyā al-Tādifī al-Ḥanbalī, *Qalā'id al-Jawāhir*, 11.
235. Sha'rānī, *al-Ṭabaqāt al-Kubrā*, 2:188.
236. Aḥmad, *Musnad*, 26287, 26298; Ibn Abī 'Āṣim, *al-Sunna*, 317.
237. Aḥmad, *Musnad*, 20318; 'Abd al-Razzāq, *Muṣannaf*, 6001; Bayhaqī, *Shu'ab al-Īmān*, 2294.
238. Ibn Māja, *Sunan: kitāb al-adab, bāb faḍl al-ḥāmidīn*, 3799.
239. Bukhārī, *Ṣaḥīḥ: kitāb bad' al-khalq, bāb dhikr al-malā'ika*, 3207.
240. Azraqī, *Akhbār Makka*, 8.
241. Ibid. 32.
242. Qur'ān, *Sūra Maryam*, 19:29–33.
243. Bukhārī, *Ṣaḥīḥ: kitāb aḥādīth al-Anbiyā', bāb qawl Allāh wa'dhkur fi'l-kitāb Maryam*, 3181.
244. Abū Dāwūd, *Sunan: kitāb al-jihād, bāb mā yu'mar bih min al-qiyām 'alā al-dawāb wa'l-bahā'im*, 2186.
245. Bayhaqī, *Dalā'il al-Nubuwwa*, 2285; Abū Nu'aym, *Dalā'il al-Nubuwwa*, Ch. 18, 266.

246. Al-Aṣbahānī, *Dalā'il al-Nubuwwa*, Ch. 18, 265.
247. ʿAbd al-Razzāq, *Muṣannaf*, 6485–86.
248. Bayhaqī, *Dalā'il al-Nubuwwa*, 2293; Bazzār, *Musnad*, 3245; Abū Nuʿaym al-Aṣbahānī, *Maʿrifat-al-Ṣaḥāba*, 3102; Ibn Ḥajar, *al-Maṭālib al-ʿĀliya, Safina, Abū ʿAbd al-Raḥmān, Mawlā Rasūl Allāh, ṣalla'llāhu ʿalayh wa sallam*, 4192.
249. Ibn Saʿd, *Ṭabaqāt, al-Juz' al-Mutammim*, 206; Ibn ʿAbd al-Barr, *al-Istīʿāb fī Maʿrifat al-Aṣḥāb*, 1:331.
250. Muḥammad ibn Yaḥyā al-Tādifī al-Ḥanbalī, *Qalā'id al-Jawāhir*, 8.
251. Qur'ān, *Sūra al-Naml*, 27:16–28.
252. Shaʿrānī, *al-Ṭabaqāt al-Kubrā*, 2:21.
253. Tirmidhī, *Sunan: kitāb al-manāqib, bāb fī ayāt ithbāt nubuwwat al-nabī*
254. Muslim, *Ṣaḥīḥ: kitāb al-faḍā'il*, 4222.
255. Bazzār, *Musnad*, 308; Bayhaqī, *Dalā'il al-Nubuwwa*, 458.
256. Bukhārī, *Ṣaḥīḥ: kitāb al-manāqib, bāb ʿalāmāt al-nubuwwa fi'l-Islām*, 3319–20.
257. Abū Dāwūd, *Sunan: kitāb al-diyāt, bāb fī man saqā rajul simm aw aṭʿamah famāt, ayuqād minh*, 3911.
258. Ṭabarānī, *Kabīr*, 2322; Bayhaqī, *Dalā'il al-Nubuwwa*, 15927.
259. Bukhārī, *Ṣaḥīḥ: kitāb al-manāqib, bāb ʿalāmāt al-nubuwwa fi'l-Islām*, 3314.
260. Qur'ān, *Sūra al-Isrā'*, 17:44.
261. Qur'ān, *Sūra al-Nūr*, 24:41.
262. Qur'ān, *Sūra Saba'*, 34:10.
263. Ṭabarānī, *Awsaṭ*, 1298; Abū Nuʿaym, *Dalā'il al-Nubuwwa*, 327.
264. Bukhārī, *Ṣaḥīḥ: kitāb al-manāqib, bāb ʿalāmāt al-nubuwwa fi'l-Islām*, 3579.
265. Qushayrī, *Risāla*, 13.
266. Bukhārī, *Ṣaḥīḥ: kitāb al-wuḍū', bāb min al-kabā'ir an lā yastatir min bawlih*, 216.
267. Aḥmad, *Musnad*, 12072, 13223; al-Ḥākim, *Mustadrak: kitāb al-Īmān*, 107; Bukhārī, *al-Adab al-Mufrad*, 883, Bazzār, *Musnad*, 3304.
268. Ṭabarānī, *Kabīr*, 954–55.
269. Qur'ān, *Sūra al-Nisā'*, 4:64.
270. Nawawī, *Majmūʿ*, 8:217, and *al-Adhkār*, 574; Ibn Kathīr, *Tafsīr*, 2:347–48.
271. Al-Muttaqī al-Hindī, *Kanz al-ʿUmmāl: al-faṣl al-thālith fī ziyārat al-qubūr*, 42556, 42602; Tammām, *Fawā'id*, 132; Ibn Abī'l-Dunyā, *Kitāb al-Qubūr*.
272. Bayhaqī, *Shuʿab al-Īmān: faṣl fī ziyārat al-qubūr*, 8989.
273. Muslim, *Ṣaḥīḥ: kitāb al-Janna wa ṣifat naʿīmaha wa ahlaha, bāb ʿarḍ maqʿad al-mayyit min al-Janna aw al-Nār ʿalayh*, 2867–68.
274. Ibid. 2869.

275. Ibn Abi'l-Dunyā, *Hawātif al-Jinān*, 99.

276. Al-Muttaqī al-Hindī, *Kanz al-ʿUmmāl*, 37261: *Musnad Ṭalḥa ibn ʿUbayd Allāh.*

277. Tirmidhī, *Sunan: kitāb faḍā'il al-Qur'ān, bāb mā jā' fī faḍl Sūra al-Mulk*, 2890.

278. Dārimī, *Sunan*, 3473.

279. Ibn ʿAsākir, *Tārīkh Dimashq*, 45:450.

280. Ṭabarī, *Tahdhīb al-Āthār*, 187.

281. Ibid. 186.

282. Bā-ʿAlawī, *al-Mashraʿ*, 2:136.

283. Shaʿrānī, *al-Ṭabaqāt al-Kubrā*, 2:111.

284. Ibid. 2:154.

285. Ibid. 2:99.

286. Ibid. 2:118.

287. Ibid. 2:133.

288. Aḥmad Muḥammad Ḥijāb, *al-ʿIẓa wa'l-Iʿtibār: rā' fī Ḥayāt al-Sayyid al-Badawī al-Dunyawiyya wa Ḥayātuh al-Barzakhiyya*, (Cairo: Dār al-Ḥusayn al-Islāmiyya, 1429/2008, second edition), 13.

289. Aḥmad Muḥammad Ḥijāb, *Al-ʿIẓa wa'l-Iʿtibār*, 25.

290. Muḥammad ibn Zayn ibn Sumayṭ, *Ghāyat al-Qaṣd wa'l-Murād fī Manāqib al-Imām al-Ḥaddād*, 1:358–59.

291. Bazzār, *Musnad*, 1702.

292. Bukhārī, *Ṣaḥīḥ: kitāb al-janā'iz, bāb al-mayyit yasmaʿ khafq al-niʿāl*, 1338.

293. Suyūṭī, *Bushrā al-Ka'īb bi Liqā' al-Ḥabīb*, Ibn ʿAbd al-Barr, *Tamhīd*; Ibn Abī al-Dunyā, *al-Qubūr*.

294. Al-Muttaqī al-Hindī, *Kanz al-ʿUmmāl*, 42556, 42602; Tammām, *Fawā'id*, 132; Ibn ʿAsākir, *Tārīkh Dimashq*, 10:380; al-Khatīb, *Tārīkh Baghdād*, 6:135; 23:295.

295. Bukhārī, *Ṣaḥīḥ: kitāb al-janā'iz, bāb mā jā' fī ʿadhāb al-qabr*, 1374.

296. Ibn al-Qayyim, *al-Rūḥ*, 9.

297. Abū Yaʿlā, *Musnad*, 6449; Ibn Ḥajar, *al-Maṭālib al-ʿāliya: bāb ʿalāmāt al-sāʿa*, 4628.

298. Shaʿrānī, *al-Ṭabaqāt al-Kubrā*, 2:100.

299. Shaʿrānī, *al-Ṭabaqāt al-Kubrā*, 2:147.

300. *Sayyid* Muḥammad ibn Zayn ibn Sumayṭ, *Ghāyat al-qaṣd wa'l-Murād*, 1:358–9.

301. Bayhaqī, *Shuʿab al-Īmān*, 10590–92. ʿAbd al-Razzāq, *Muṣannaf*, 20114; Ṭabarānī, *Kabīr*, 3289; Ibn Ḥajar al-ʿAsqalānī, *al-Iṣāba fī Maʿrifat al-Ṣaḥāba: dhikr man ismuh al-Ḥārith*, 1:196.

302. Bazzār, *Musnad*, 1702; al-Ḥārith ibn Usāma, *Musnad: kitāb ʿalāmāt al-nubuwwa, bāb fī ḥayātih wa wafātih*, 943; Ibn Ḥajar, *al-Maṭālib al-ʿāliya: kitāb al-manāqib, bāb*

barakātih ṣalla Allāh ʿalayh was sallam ḥayyan wa mayyitan, 3925.

303. Bayhaqī, *Shuʿab al-Īmān*, 2896; Ṭabarānī, *Kabīr*, 772.
304. Ṭabarānī, *Awsaṭ*, 246, 4070.
305. Abū Dāwūd, *Sunan: kitāb al-ṣalāt, bāb faḍl yawm al-jumʿa wa laylat al-jumʿa*, 883; *bāb al-istighfār*, 1308; Nasāʾī, *Sunan: kitāb al- jumʿa, bāb ikthār al-ṣalā ʿalā al-Nabī yawm al- jumʿa*, 1357.
306. Ibn al-Mubārak, *al-Zuhd waʾl-Raqāʾiq*, 1778; Qurʾān, *Sūra al-Nisāʾ*, 4:41.
307. Aḥmad, *Musnad*, 12222; Ṭabarānī, *Kabīr*, 3791; *Awsaṭ*, 152; Bayhaqī, *Shuʿab al-Īmān*, 9876; Ṭabarī, *Tahdhīb al-Āthār*, 182; Ṭayālīsī, *Musnad*, 1894.
308. Aḥmad, *Musnad*, 12222; Ṭabarānī, *Kabīr*, 3791, and *Awsaṭ*, 152.
309. Al-Ḥākim, *Mustadrak: kitāb al-riqāq*, 7960; Bayhaqī, *Shuʿab al-Īmān: faṣl wa mimmā yalḥaq biʾl-ṣabr ʿind al-maṣāʾib*, 9876.
310. Abū Dāwūd, *Sunan: kitāb al-zuhd, bāb min khabar Abiʾl-Dardāʾ*, 211; Ibn al-Mubārak, *al-Zuhd*, 1777; Ibn Abiʾl-Dunyā, *al-Manāmāt*, 5.
311. Abū Nuʿaym, *Ḥilyat al-Awliyāʾ*, 4:254; Ibn al-Jawzī, *Ṣifat al-Ṣafwa*, 1:484.
312. Ibn Abiʾl-Dunyā, *al-Manāmāt*, 18.
313. Muslim, *Ṣaḥīḥ: kitāb al-Īmān, bāb adnā ahl al-Janna manzila fihā*, 277.
314. Qurʾān, *Sūra Yā-Sīn*, 36:65.
315. Ibn Abī Shayba, *Muṣannaf*, 3:125; Ibn Abīʾl-Dunyā, *al-Muḥtaḍirīn*, 8; Abū Dāwūd, *Marāsīl*, 385, attributed to the Prophet, not to ʿUmar; Bayhaqī, *Shuʿab al-Īmān*, 4019.
316. Suyūṭī, *Sharḥ al-Ṣudūr bi Sharḥ Ḥāl al-Mawtā waʾl-Qubūr*, 60.
317. Ibid. 60.
318. ʿAbd al-Razzāq, *Muṣannaf*, 6142.
319. Ibn ʿAsākir, *Tārīkh Dimashq*, 58:447–48.
320. Ibn Abī Shayba, *Muṣannaf*, 8:225.
321. Ibn Abiʾl-Dunyā, *al-Muḥtaḍirīn*, 348.
322. Suyūṭī, *Sharḥ al-Ṣudūr*, 99.
323. Ibn ʿAsākir, *Tārīkh Dimashq*, 45:254.
324. Qurʾān, *Sūra al-Qaṣaṣ*, 28:83.
325. Ibn Kathīr, *al-Bidāya waʾl-Nihāya*, 9:235.
326. Ibn ʿAsākir, *Tārīkh Dimashq*, 56:174.
327. Qurʾān, *Sūra al-Nisāʾ*, 4:69.
328. Dhahabī, *Manāqib Abī Ḥanīfa*, 32.
329. Qurʾān, *Sūra al-Qiyāma*, 75:13
330. Suyūṭī, *Sharḥ al-Ṣudūr*, 109.
331. Ibn Abī Shayba, *Kitāb al-Zuhd: kalām Ibrāhīm al-Taymī*, 8.

332. Ibn Abī Ya'lā, *Ṭabaqāt al-Ḥanābila: 'Uthmān ibn 'Īsā al-Zāhid*, 2:170.

333. Suyūṭī, *Sharḥ al-Ṣudūr*, 120.

334. Qur'ān, *Sūra al-Tawbah*, 9:21-22

335. Abū Bakr ibn Muḥammad al-Shillī Bā-'Alawī, *al-Mashra' al-Rawī*, 2:15. The verses are from Qur'ān, *Sūra al-Tawba*, 9:21–22 Abū Bakr ibn Muḥammad al-Shillī Bā-'Alawī, al-Mashra' al-Rawī, 2:15. The verses are from Qur'ān, Sūra al-Tawba, 9:21–22.

336. Bukhārī, *Ṣaḥīḥ: kitāb al-janā'iz, bāb al-mayyit yasma' khafq al-ni'āl*, 1338.

337. Tirmidhī, *Sunan: kitāb al-janā'iz, bāb mā jā' fī 'adhāb al-qabr*, 1071; Bayhaqī, *Shu'ab al-Īmān*, 423; Ṭabarānī. *Kabīr*, 993.

338. Bukhārī, *Ṣaḥīḥ: kitāb al-janā'iz, bāb al-mayyit yasma' khafq al-ni'āl*, 1338.

339. Tirmidhī, *Sunan: kitāb ṣifat al-Qiyāma, bāb mā jā' fī ṣifat awāni al-ḥawḍ*, 2460.

340. Muslim, *Ṣaḥīḥ: kitāb al-Janna wa ṣifat na'īmaha wa ahlaha, bāb 'Arḍ maq'ad al-mayyit min al-Janna aw al-Nār 'alayh*, 2866.

341. Tirmidhī, *Sunan: kitāb al-janā'iz, bāb mā jā' fī 'adhāb al-qabr*, 1071.

342. Ibn 'Asākir, *Tārīkh Dimashq*, 58:378; Abū Nu'aym, *Ḥilyat al-Awliyā'*, 3:127.

343. Ṭabarānī, *Kabīr*, 90; Ibn al-Mubārak, *al-Zuhd*, 250.

344. Wāqidī, *Maghāzī*, 1:210; Ibn Sa'd, *Ṭabaqāt*, 3:431.

345. Ibid.

346. Ibn Ḥibbān, *Ṣaḥīḥ: al-bayān bi ann daghṭat al-qabr la yanjū minhā aḥad min hādhihi'l-umma*, 3177; Aḥmad, *Musnad*, 23148, 23522; Ṭabarānī, *Kabīr*, 12801, 13379.

347. Aḥmad, *Musnad: Musnad al-Anṣār, Ḥadīth Ḥudhayfa ibn al-Yamān*, 14344, 14498; Ṭabarānī, *Kabīr*, 5208.

348. Aḥmad, *Musnad*, 23457.

349. Bayhaqī, *Dalā'il al-Nubuwwa*, 2967.

350. Ṭabarānī, *Awsaṭ*, 7128; Abū Nu'aym al-Aṣbahānī, *Ma'rifat al-Ṣaḥāba*, 272.

351. Muslim, *Ṣaḥīḥ: kitāb al-janā'iz, bāb al-ṣalā 'alā al-qabr*, 1588; Ibn Māja, *Sunan: kitāb al-janā'iz, bāb mā jā' fī'l-ṣalā 'alā al-qabr*, 1528–29.

352. Ibn Abi'l-Dunyā, *Kitāb al-Tahajjud wa Qiyām al-Layl*, 152, 411.

353. Ibid. 153.

354. Abū Nu'aym, *Ḥilyat al-Awliyā'*, 1:356; Ṭabarī, *Tahdhīb al-Āthār*, 188; Ibn Abi'l-Dunyā, *Kitāb al-Tahajjud*, 413.

355. Ibn Ḥibbān, *Ṣaḥīḥ*, 3187.

356. Ibn 'Asākir, *Tārīkh Dimashq*, 24:356; Dhahabī, *Siyar A'lām al-Nubalā'*, 4:95–96.

357. Quoted by Suyūṭī in *Bushrā al-Ka'īb bi Liqā' al-Ḥabīb*, 113, and attributed to Daylamī's *Musnad al-Firdaws*.

358. Aḥmad ibn Ḥanbal, *al-Zuhd*, 1:359.

359. Suyūṭī, *Sharḥ al-Ṣudūr*, 138.

360. Ibid. 139.

361. Ibid. 139.

362. Qur'ān, *Sūra al-Baqara*, 2:33–35.

363. Ibid. 2:37.

364. Qur'ān, *Sūra al-Shūrā*, 42:51.

365. Qur'ān, *Sūra Ṭā-Hā*, 20:11–48.

366. Qur'ān, *Sūra al-Aʿrāf*, 7:142.

367. Tirmidhī, *Sunan: kitāb tafsīr al-Qur'ān, bāb wa min Sūra Āl-ʿImrān*, 3010.

368. Bukhārī, *Ṣaḥīḥ: kitāb al-tawḥid, bāb mā jā' fī qawl Allāh taʿāla: Wujūh yawm idh nāḍira ilā rabbiha nādhira*, 7005.

369. Azraqī, *Akhbār Makka*, 34.

370. Bukhārī, *Ṣaḥīḥ: kitāb al-tafsīr, bāb qawlih wa taqūlu hal min mazīd*, 4850.

371. Bukhārī, *Ṣaḥīḥ: kitāb al-ṣalāt, bāb al-ibrād bi'l-dhuhr fī shiddat al-ḥarr*, 533.

372. Qur'ān, *Sūra al-Qiyāma*, 75:22–23.

373. Bukhārī, *Ṣaḥīḥ: kitāb al-tawḥīd, bāb mā jā' fī qawl Allāh taʿāla: Wujūh yawm idh nāḍira ilā rabbiha nādhira*, 7434.

374. Bukhārī, *Ṣaḥīḥ: kitāb al-tawḥīd, bāb mā jā' fī qawl Allāh taʿāla: Wujūh yawm idh nāḍira ilā rabbiha nādhira*, 7437.

375. Qur'ān, *Sūra Yūnus*, 10:26.

376. Tirmidhī, *Sunan: kitāb ṣifat al-Janna, bāb mā jā' fī ru'yat al-rabb*, 2552.

377. Ghazālī, *Iḥyā' ʿUlūm al-Dīn*, 2:242.

378. Bukhārī, *Ṣaḥīḥ: kitāb al-janā'iz, bāb al-rajul yanʿā ilā ahl al-mayyit bi nafsih*, 1246.

379. Ibid. 1245.

380. Ṭabarānī, *Kabīr*, 13587, 13588; Bayhaqī, *Dalā'il al-Nubuwwa*, 1009.

381. Bayhaqī, *Dalā'il al-Nubuwwa*, 1011.

382. Ibn Saʿd, *Ṭabaqāt*, 3:194.

383. Al-Muḥibb al-Ṭabarī, *al-Riyāḍ al-Naḍira fī Manāqib al-ʿAshara*, 1:214; Ibn al-Qayyim, *al-Rūḥ*, 244; Ghazālī, *Iḥyā'*, 2:227.

384. Ibn al-Qayyim, *al-Rūḥ*, 197.

385. Qushayrī, *Risāla: bāb al-firāsa*, 106.

386. Ibid. 108.

387. Nabhānī, *Jāmiʿ Karāmāt al-Awliyā'*, 2:56.

388. Ibn ʿAṭā'illāh, *Laṭā'if al-Minan*, 162.

389. Bā-ʿAlawī, *al-Mashraʿ*, 2:136.

390. Shaʿrānī, *al-Ṭabaqāt al-Kubrā*, 2:94.

391. Ibid. 2:104.

392. Ibid.

393. Ibid. 2:106.

394. Ḥijāb, *al-ʿIẓa wa'l-Iʿtibār*, 111–12.

395. Ibn ʿArabī, *al-Futūḥāt al-Makkiyya*, 2:464–65.

396. Shaʿrānī, *al-Ṭabaqāt al-Kubrā*, 2:89.

397. Shaʿrānī, *al-Ṭabaqāt al-Ṣughrā*, 98.

398. Ibid. 69.

399. Shaʿrānī, *al-Ṭabaqāt al-Ṣughrā*, 93.

400. Ibn Abī Shayba, *Muṣannaf: kitāb al-Īmān wa'l-ru'yā*, 7:244; Aḥmad ibn Ḥanbal, *Kitāb al-Zuhd*, 1145.

401. Bayhaqī, *Dalā'il al-Nubuwwa: bāb al-Isrā' bi Rasūl Allāh*, 654; Ṭabarī, *Tahdhīb al-Āthār*, 2757.

402. Bayhaqī, *Dalā'il al-Nubuwwa: bāb al-Isrā' bi Rasūl Allāh*, 677; Ṭabarī, *Tahdhīb al-Āthār*, 2766.

403. Qushayrī, *Risāla: bāb karāmāt al-awliyā'*, 1:289.

404. Muḥammad ibn Yaḥyā al-Tādifī al-Ḥanbalī, *Qalā'id al-Jawāhir*, 10.

405. Bayhaqī, *Shuʿab al-Īmān*, 10271.

406. Bukhārī, *Ṣaḥīḥ: kitāb aḥādīth al-Anbiyā', bāb dhikr Idrīs ʿalayh al-salām*, 3342.

407. Bukhārī, *Ṣaḥīḥ: kitāb al-tafsīr, bāb qawluh: Alladhīn yuḥsharūn ʿalā wujūhihim ilā Jahannam*, 4760.

408. Muslim, *Ṣaḥīḥ: kitāb al-zuhd wa'l-raqā'iq, bāb ʿuqubat man ya'mur bi'l-maʿrūf wa lā yafʿaluh wa yanhā ʿan al-munkar wa yafʿaluh*, 2989.

409. Qur'ān, *Sūra al-Ṭalāq*, 65:12.

410. Qur'ān, *Sūra al-Sajda*, 32:5.

411. ʿAbd al-Razzāq, *Muṣannaf*, 8875; Azraqī, *Akhbār Makka*, 37.

412. Tirmidhī, *Sunan: kitāb ṣifat al-Qiyāma*, 2460.

413. Qur'ān, *Sūra al-Isrā'*, 17:44.

414. Bukhārī, *Ṣaḥīḥ: kitāb bad' al-khalq, bāb ṣifat al-shams wa'l-qamar bi ḥusbān*, 3199. The verse is from the Qur'ān, *Sūra Yā-Sīn*, 36:38.

a HIGHER

Mar

ISLAMIC • VILLAGE